Half a World Away

HALF A WORLD AWAY

Living the Dream in a Land Down Under

Alistair McGuinness

Bongo Books

Half a World Away Copyright © 2015 by A McGuinness.

CONTENTS

1.	Acknowledgments	1
2.	Living the dream	2
3.	The barbeque	6
4.	The boat	18
5.	Mushrooms	37
6.	A job for life	47
7.	A new Australian	54
8.	Walkabout	57
9.	Sunshine and Shadow	104
10.	Half a world away	106
11.	In a stew	110
12.	Dreamtime	126
13.	Long hot summer	150
14.	Sunrise	156
15.	The bridge	161
16.	The price of iron ore	167
17.	Micro adventures	179
18.	Authors Note	185
19.	About Alistair	187
20.	Gap Year Travel	189

1

ACKNOWLEDGMENTS

These stories are dedicated to my wife, Fran and sister, Alice. To move from one country to another is a life changing decision and Fran has constantly helped me embrace and enjoy our new life in Australia.

Alice travelled to Australia to support Fran during her first pregnancy, but never met our second child. She was involved in a tragic accident and passed away in 2006, a few months before he was born. We often feel her presence and miss her so much!

A big thank you goes to Jenny Warr, for the quirky illustrations and to packardimages.com.au for the image of Sydney Harbour Bridge and the stunning cover designs.

2

LIVING THE DREAM

"All our dreams can come true, if we have the courage to pursue them."
Walt Disney

2006. Ningaloo Reef, Western Australia.

There it was again. I knew it wasn't my imagination after all. I could see it clearly now, just at the edge of the reef, its fin gliding easily through the clear water. Each time it circled, it seemed to edge closer and my initial euphoria at spotting the creature was now replaced by short, sharp breaths as I contemplated escape. I broke the surface and sucked greedily through the snorkel, ignoring the trickle of warm salt water oozing down my throat while I cleared fog from my diving mask.

I dipped my head below the water again and checked for its whereabouts but was momentarily distracted by the abundance of activity. Schools of brightly coloured fish nibbled on pristine coral and an octopus was in transit along the seabed, changing colour as it drifted across the sandy bottom. For a few minutes I snorkelled near the surface, seemingly ignored by the fish that swam past, always just out of reach.

I sensed rather than saw the large sea creature looming to my right. I turned sharply and found myself face-to-face with a loggerhead turtle, its hollowed eyes looking into mine. With apparent ease, it changed direction and headed into deeper water. Instinctively I surface-dived and kicked hard to keep up, but the turtle was too quick and disappeared into an abyss, leaving me alone once more.

That's when I saw the shape again, closer now, in search of prey. I knew what it was. The dense body, steely eyes, rippled torso and black-tipped fin meant only one thing and with every flick of its tail it edged closer.

Blacktip reef shark

My breathing quickened and I lifted my head above the water to check the distance to the beach. I was ridiculously close and could hear children's laughter wafting on the summer breeze, which prompted me to search for my wife, Fran, among the sparse group of holidaymakers enjoying the sunshine. I could see her sitting near the water's edge scooping sand into a plastic bucket, and cajoling our two young boys into play. I flapped my arms and with a sixth sense she looked up and called out, "Hey boys, there's Daddy, give him a wave."

They looked up from their sandcastle and called out, but I was too preoccupied to enjoy their spontaneous greetings. As they waved, I inhaled deeply through the snorkel and with dignified stealth kicked hard towards the beach. As my fins thrashed hastily on the surface, I glanced left and right, hoping that our Ningaloo Reef guide book had been correct and that blacktip reef sharks rarely attacked. The warm water shallowed to my knees and I stood to call out to Fran, but a strong current had pulled me further down the shoreline and the warm breeze snatched my taut words.

Between the beach and me was a four-metre-wide channel of deep water and with a determined leap I plunged into the middle. Being so near to land I suddenly felt very safe and wallowed for a few seconds, allowing the current to drift me parallel with the shoreline. That's when I saw the shark for the third time, its fin slicing through the water as it sped through the channel. There was no time to react and as my body tensed, it brushed its coarse tail across my stomach and dived below the waterline. I scrambled onto the beach and lay on the searing sand, gasping for breath and grinning with excitement.

Being circled by sharks was not something they had

mentioned at the migration seminar in the UK a few years earlier. The packed auditorium had been filled with hopeful migrants listening to talks about living in Australia, where balmy evenings under the Southern Cross were part of the adventure of starting a new life Down Under. But those glossy presentations to thousands of hopefuls now seemed a lifetime ago. Moving from one country to another is a major life event and every family has stories to tell. I have picked a few of ours.

3

THE BARBEQUE

"There are far better things ahead than any we leave behind."
C.S. Lewis
2003. Bedfordshire, England.

Bright sunshine streamed through the bedroom window and as I gazed over the slate rooftops, there was not a hint of cloud in the pale blue sky. It was the first sunny morning in months and the unexpected warmth seemed to give the neighbourhood a boost after a long drawn-out winter. During breakfast with Fran, a trip to the garden centre was discussed and by late afternoon our patio was once more in bloom, with each terracotta pot filled with fresh potting mix and colourful wildflowers. We also purchased bags of charcoal in anticipation of numerous farewell barbeques. These would prepare us for those lazy days of summer, when Australians embrace outdoor living and spend more time socialising in their alfresco than sitting in their lounge rooms watching television. Our friends thought we were mad. Not about emigrating, but about wasting money on potted plants and herb gardens when we were leaving home to live in Australia.

But we wanted this spring and summer to feel special, as it might be our last in England for a long time. Maybe forever. Our world had recently been turned upside down with General Motors planning to close the Luton Vauxhall car factory and I would soon be made redundant. After three decades living in England it felt like the right time to find our place in the sun. Our first stop would be South America, followed by Africa and many months later, Australia, to start a new life Down Under. But before we departed from Heathrow there were so many things we wanted to do and so many places we wanted to explore.

Spring and summer raced by as we traversed the country on weekends away and spent precious moments at home with family and friends. Any remaining time was spent at work, as valuable overtime meant the chance to save for the gap year adventure before touching down in Australia. As announced, the factory gates finally closed and I was made redundant in late summer. Before we departed, the only thing remaining on our list was to have a barbeque at home.

With August all but over, there was only one weekend left before our one-way trip to the airport, and the Indian summer promised by the weather man had failed to materialise. I ventured into the back garden and gazed up at the sky to gauge the chance of rain. Two small patches of blue were visible in the thick band of mottled cloud that drifted far above the rooftops. Any blue sky, no matter how insignificant, meant hope. I dragged the portable barbeque out of the garden shed, set it down on the patio and went in search of ingredients.

Cracked pepper sausages were on special at Tescos and a late summer crop of tomatoes on the vine complemented the iceberg lettuce and farm-fresh cucumbers. On the way to the checkout I searched for a six-pack of Australian beer and dropped the warm cans into the shopping trolley. I had once heard that Australians bought beer without leaving their cars, with drive-through bottle shops a common sight across the country. That was all in the future. What mattered right now was getting the barbeque lit.

As the checkout girl scanned my purchases I felt myself daydreaming once again at the thought of what lay ahead. If all went to plan we would finally discover what makes Australia such a sought-after country. There seemed to be so many stories about deadly wildlife, the laid-back lifestyle and beachside living and I was keen to discover the truth. Were there really funnel-web spiders under every toilet seat in Sydney? Did Australians really say "G'day" and "No worries"? I had so many unanswered questions about their way of life. Surely they didn't have barbeques every day?

The last few weeks had been tense and emotional, with my life in England coming to a close and somewhere shrouded in the unknown lay a new life in a foreign land. Each morning I would wake with a jolt, instantly aware that departure was a day nearer and would spend the day flushed with excitement. Each evening the demons arrived as thoughts of leaving behind my elderly father played on my mind. I knew he would adore the sunshine when he visited but somehow this didn't seem to justify our need to move half a world away.

During the drive back from the shops I took a detour past my childhood house. Littlefield Road hadn't changed much over the years. The council houses looked slightly worn and in need of a makeover, but most lawns were lush, with colourful flowerbeds along their edges. What had changed was The Green, a small oval where I used to play football after school with neighbourhood friends. Established trees now skirted the perimeter and the council had added parking bays, making the grass area smaller. I wondered if the local children still played football on The Green, using jumpers as goalposts, but there were none around to ask.

I stopped the car outside my old house, catching a faint smell of spices in the cool breeze as the new owners prepared dinner. I wanted to knock at the familiar door and be invited in, but it wouldn't be the same. Not anymore. This was their home now and my childhood was over. It was time to move on.

I ran onto the grass then stood in the centre of the oval where the improvised goals used to be and closed my eyes, hearing Mum's voice calling from the doorway, telling me that dinner was ready. But that was all a long time ago and her gentle voice was now just a distant memory. All I heard was the faint sound of a dog barking and the hearty chuckle of laughter cascading through an open window. I fought back tears and drove to my terraced house, not knowing when I would next return to the place of my childhood.

As I neared home, the roads narrowed. They were lined with parked cars and time and time again I pulled into tight gaps to allow traffic to pass by. But my days of navigating these familiar streets were coming to an end. Within a month we would be working as conservation volunteers in the Amazon jungle and a year from now hoped to be driving along remote outback roads, under endless blue skies.

My street was also filled with parked cars. Both sides, lined bumper to bumper, which forced me up the hill in search of a vacant space. Maybe our future house in Australia would have a driveway with a garage. The thought of living near the ocean prompted a hearty chuckle and I found myself singing as I walked home.

Once inside, I placed the groceries in the kitchen and made my way into our back garden. Over the years we had splashed out on a paved patio, and decorated it with colourful pots, a funky set of wooden chairs and a small wooden table. But no amount of knick-knacks could take away the fact that our little piece of England was hemmed in on all sides by century-old houses.

My terraced street

With no high fences between the elongated back gardens, privacy was a rare event. I had always enjoyed standing in our garden and chatting about the weather with neighbours five houses away. But the downfall of such intimacy was the lack of privacy. Maybe when the houses were built in the early twentieth century, this type of behaviour was normal. But after three decades of waving to neighbours while watering plants or sunbathing, I was ready for a change. I guess the easy solution would have been to move house, and before the factory announced its closure we were actively searching for a home in the country. But the lure of travel and the opportunity to live in Australia was too strong and the chance to live in an English village was forgotten amongst the euphoria.

The cool afternoon seemed to have impacted on the neighbourhood gardeners and I found myself alone as I poured coals on the hot plate and doused them in lighter fuel. There was no sign of blue in the sky anymore but I felt committed now and decided it was time for music and refreshments. As I cracked opened a can of Fosters, I heard the distinct shuffle of slippers on concrete as my next-door neighbour came outside to investigate.

John was long into retirement. He had served in the army during the latter part of World War Two and then worked for the post office up until he had earned a gold watch for long service. He was short and stocky and blessed with a trimmed thatch of grey hair. Now over eighty, his faculties and wit were still intact and his sharp blue eyes rarely missed anything new that had been added to our patio collection.

He let me prepare my music collection and as the distinctive sound of Brit Pop pulsated gently from the speakers, he ambled closer to the mesh fence.

"What's that racket, Ali?"

"It's Oasis, John. It's the kind of music you play in summer. You know. To get you in the mood for barbeques." He stared past me, his eyes locked onto the speakers and called out, "I can't hear what you're saying with all that noise."

I turned the volume down, so that it now resembled background music in a coffee shop and asked, "How's that?"

"Much better."

Then he pointed to the barbeque standing nearby.

"What's that for?"

I knew he was aware. It was a game we played every time something new appeared in our garden. He had survived the blitz then watched as the demographics that made up the neighbourhood changed from long-term families to transient workers, bed-sitters and first-time owners. He was still bemused by my decision to paint our garden shed bright blue. Time and time again he had come out to investigate as I splashed colourful paint across the aged timbers.

"Sheds aren't meant to be blue. They're always brown. It looks daft if you ask me."

As I stood halfway up the stepladder, I would smile and wave back, "I've got some spare paint if you need it, John. I'll come over later if you want and can spruce up yours. Blue sheds are all the rage, you know!"

"Not on your nelly, mate," he would quickly reply before heading inside for his afternoon cuppa.

That had been last year and it was still a topic he liked to raise. I enjoyed our little chats over the fence, but it was clear we were eons apart. He was never going to move away and often reminisced about the past. I was looking only to the future and had grown weary of the street. There was nowhere to park, each new neighbour was less friendly than the last and the back gardens were only wide enough to swing a kitten. My latest neighbours on the other side were refugees from Zimbabwe. At first they seemed harmless enough and knocks on the door to ask for sugar seemed somehow quaint. That's what neighbours have always done and we gave graciously. We even invited them round for tea and biscuits. But the house of two people soon became five, then eight and just lately the rising damp from their overgrown back garden was souring international relations. I also sensed a sugar embargo coming on unless they removed the double mattress and broken settee from the shared alleyway.

John pulled me from my daydream as he pointed to the sky and called out, "Have you seen those dark clouds? There's rain on the way. I hope you've got an umbrella." I dismissed his remarks with a nonchalant shrug, but deep down sensed disaster. As I reached for my beer I turned my face towards the skyline. The only blue I could see now was my garden shed and apart from green grass, every other colour looked grey and depressing. In the distance a thin band of dark clouds formed, slowly moving across the horizon towards my patio. I turned my attention back to John, "Do you fancy a sausage later? They're special ones, with cracked pepper and organic herbs." He looked at the gathering clouds and replied, "Why don't you just grill them in the kitchen like normal people?"

"I'm practising for Australia, John. Apparently you have to prove to the Government that you can barbeque effectively. Otherwise they won't let you in."

He ignored my humour and watched inquisitively as match after match failed to light the coals. I drenched them in more fuel, grabbed another beer and offered one to John but he wasn't interested and stood watching as I struggled to light the charcoal. Somehow the second lager didn't seem to taste as refreshing as the first. Maybe the frustration of trying to light the coals had dulled my taste buds.

I could still feel John's presence as he foraged in his nurtured gardens for any weeds that may have sprouted overnight. I contemplated lighting a newspaper from the kitchen stove and running into the back garden to hurl it onto the saturated coals, but realised this was desperate thinking.

"Ali, have you seen the rain clouds? They're getting nearer and you haven't got a flame yet." I smiled, but deep down felt a sudden urge to scream.

Just then the cool wind dropped and a whooshing

sound from the barbeque was followed by a sharp crackle as the fuel ignited, releasing a hazy blue fireball into the air.

"Well, that took ages, didn't it?" I heard from afar, but I was too elated to reply and raced inside for the sausages, returning also with a thick jumper and an umbrella. The meat grilled slowly as a fine layer of mist descended on the neighborhood and once again I was alone in the garden.

Fran arrived at dusk, armed with a bottle of wine, and we sat outside in the fading light, determined to experience at least one outdoor meal before summer ended. Protected by our umbrella, we ignored the light drizzle falling from the granite skies and concentrated instead, on the final preparations for migration.

We would miss John and his quirky ways. His petite wife, Wynn, had always been generous, with homemade cakes on offer whenever we popped around for afternoon tea. But those days were soon to be over. We had already started packing in readiness to move to Australia. Tomorrow we would head to Milton Keynes in search of rucksacks, sleeping bags and walking boots in preparation for our worldwide trip. As the last of the summer wine finished, I gazed over the roofline, dreaming of one day cooking barbecues Down Under on warm summer evenings.

A few weeks later, the Indian summer arrived, just in time for our departure date. While walking towards the garden shed, to double check it was locked, I could hear the distinct sound of children's laughter. A young family three houses away were embracing the sunshine, with squeals from the toddlers as they trundled along the paving on their scooters while their mum unpegged yesterday's washing from the line. Her husband was watering a flowerbed, flicking droplets onto his giggling children as they raced past. He noticed me staring and waved. When they first moved in, we had exchanged names from afar, but the hectic summer had suppressed anything beyond the occasional back garden chat.

He was pointing to the cloudless sky and saying something, but his children's laughter drowned out the words. I felt like replying, "Sorry for not getting to know you more, but we're off to Australia to live in a house with an automatic garage door." I realised how conceited this would sound and instead, called out, "What amazing weather. Anyone would think we're living in Australia." A wailing child distracted his attention and as he knelt to investigate, I went back inside, just as the front door knocked. It was Fran's mum and dad, which signaled that our departure was imminent.

To embrace the autumn sunshine, two Zimbabweans from next door had dragged their discarded settee from the alleyway and placed it on the pavement. They wore Arsenal football shirts and were sprawled across the matted seat, watching cars and buses trundle by. As we emerged from the house for the final time, they raised their beer cans and wished us good luck, then giggled softly as we struggled to cram our overstuffed rucksacks into the car.

John and Wynn opened their front door to bid farewell, but never ventured onto the street. Suddenly it was all too real. Tears welled in Fran's eyes and she rushed towards them, tightly holding my hand as I ran alongside. For a few precious seconds we hugged them closely, then shook their hands and promised to stay in touch.

When we drove away from the curbside I watched John

and Wynn, as they waved from their doorway. From the back seat, I raised my hand in a farewell gesture and deep down felt a stab of guilt, as if we were abandoning them. I hoped they had plenty of sugar in the pantry, as they could expect a knock on the door from the Zimbabweans any time soon.

4

THE BOAT

"Sometimes it's the smallest decision that can change your life forever."
Keri Russell
2003. London, UK and Perth, Western Australia.

It was during the afternoon interval at the migration seminar that my *sliding door* moment occurred. The presentations were a sell-out, filled with hundreds of Brits in search of a better life in South Africa, Australia or New Zealand. Migration agents were strategically placed throughout the corridors, handing out helium-filled balloons to children in the hope of enticing their parents to discuss their plans. As we walked past the stalls, I tuned into the snippets of conversation and time and time again the same words were repeated: skills, qualifications, age and experience.

In the majority of circumstances, these key elements are the main criteria to gain entry to Australia or New Zealand, based on the amount of points you receive in each category. If you meet the standard and your skill is in demand, then you could find yourself with enough points to apply for a visa. One question constantly nagged me as I listened to intelligent people hang on to every word of the migration agents.

Was it desperation or good business sense to pay thousands of pounds to consultants, when the visa application had been simplified over the years and could even be completed online? I needed to know more and headed into a large room for the next presentation, which was called, "Five Reasons Why You Need to Live on the Sunshine Coast."

By the time the third presenter had finished his slideshow we were ready for a break and made our way to the nearest café to sit and read all the leaflets, magazines and business cards that had been handed out. I had figured by now that it was the risk of submitting the application incorrectly that turned most people to migration consultants, especially when age was a concern. The point system can change at any time, but one trend remains. The older you are, the less points you earn. One year older could mean a drop of 10 points as you move from one age category to another. A potential applicant on this precipice is a desperate person and smart migration agents can be very persuasive that applications managed by them will be successful.

While queuing for coffee I made eye contact with the man alongside me and we began chatting. Kevin was a wiry-haired electrician who had travelled down from Scunthorpe for the seminar and eagerly explained the technicalities of gaining a licence to work as an electrician in Australia. According to Kevin, it involved assessments, college exams, interstate tests and interviews. It sounded time-consuming and shrouded in bureaucracy and I was keen to find out more, but couldn't take my eyes off the blueberry muffins on display. He must have been fuelled by my enthusiastic responses and despite the fact that I was now in mid-sentence to the waitress, he handed me a colourful booklet from an earlier presentation.

The glossy picture on the first page depicted a groomed family of four enjoying a picnic barbeque in a park, overlooking an idyllic beach. He leaned forward and whispered, "They even have free barbeques. They're everywhere. Imagine that. They'd be vandalised in my street and I've had enough of traffic jams, constant rain and the unions."

As I collected the coffee, he began to ramble, his voice strained with emotion, "I want to work in the gold mines as they say you can earn a fortune, but that last migration expert told me I might be ten points short to gain a visa, due to my age."

While I sprinkled sugar into the mug, he moved even closer, his eyes wide, "Bloody stupid rule if you ask me. How can 45 be too old? I'm in my prime, you know."

Emigration is big business and there seemed to be lots of people at the seminar impatient to fast-track to a new life, including Kevin, who was beginning to make me wish I hadn't revealed my electrical trade to him. The waitress intervened and asked for his order, just as Fran called my name. It was the perfect time to escape, so I wished him luck and excused myself.

His desperation to move to Australia had unsettled me, as we didn't feel a compelling need to escape forever. All we wanted was an adventure! We had lots of friends, a caring family, didn't mind the British weather, embraced the diverse countryside and appreciated the proximity of England to mainland Europe.

But as I listened to similar conversations I sensed that

others felt the same as Kevin and wanted to make a real and lasting change to their lives. Australia seemed to be an easy answer but I couldn't help wondering if he was searching for a new life or just running away from a bad one. He was now in deep conversation with another hopeful and just as I took a nibble of my muffin, Fran called my name once more.

She was standing alongside two people and by the way she was holding the hand of woman I sensed they had met before. I quickly realised that our paths had crossed multiple times at weekend social events across Luton but this was the first time I had actually been in extended conversation with Jo and her husband John. They were early thirties, both blonde, with bright smiles and firm handshakes.

While Fran had been teaching young children and I had been carving a career with a multinational, they had been running their own successful company and had just applied for visas to run their own business in Australia. After quick hellos and a reminder of the last birthday party we had last met at, they asked where we were moving to in Australia.

This was the first time anyone had ever asked us. Fran and I exchanged looks and grinned sheepishly. We didn't know. Our prime objective was securing a visa for Australia but we hadn't thought about which city or region we might settle in. Our thoughts had been consumed by the intricacies and logistics of the upheaval and besides, our sights were also set on a backpacking adventure. This included a lifelong ambition to venture into the Amazon to work as conservation volunteers. The thought of where to live in Australia seemed a long way away.

"Perth is the place!" John exclaimed.

"We love it." Jo agreed and quickly explained, "It has a wonderful climate, with guaranteed summers. The beaches are magical, the children have wide open spaces to play in and the lifestyle is laid back compared to England."

After multiple visits they knew Australia well and over coffee they gave us numerous reasons why Perth was the pick of all the major cities. It was obvious that they were determined to move to Australia. For them, this wasn't a gap year adventure, but a permanent move to the other side of the world and it was clear they weren't in a hurry to return. John's final words as we exchanged email addresses were, "You wait and see, guys. Perth is an amazing place. Make sure you look us up when you get there. We'll look after you!" And that was our *sliding door* moment.

I knew nothing about Perth, very little about Australia beyond the brochures and in a continent the size of Russia knew four people, all of whom had left my home town of Luton a decade before. Paddy and Vince lived in Melbourne and Carmel and Mary in Brisbane. Now I knew two more and according to Jo and John, Perth was *the* best place to live in Australia.

We chose a migration agent, paid the fees and before moving to Australia, embarked on a worldwide adventure trip. While our visa application waited in a queue to be processed, we headed into the Ecuadorian jungle to plant trees and teach English, and then backpacked through Peru and Bolivia. Our worldwide trip continued with a trek to the summit of Mount Kilimanjaro and an overland trip through Southern Africa. We were chased by lions, charged by rhinos, flipped upside down on the Zambezi and threatened by taxi drivers in Johannesburg.

Our visa application was accepted while we were on the tropical island of Fiji and after a visit to the consulate; we touched down in Melbourne, as residents of Australia.

I'm not sure what we were hoping for as the baggy-eyed security officer stamped our passports at the airport. He had probably overdosed on excited migrants grinning at him at three in the morning, and waved us through with a worn smile. I hoped an Aboriginal would be sitting in the airport lounge welcoming us with a blend of traditional sounds on his didgeridoo. But the only sign of life was a bored cleaner searching for a place to hide.

Outside the terminal we stood in line for a taxi, huddling against each other as a fresh wind tore across the empty car park. A bright yellow car pulled over and we jumped inside. "Where to mate?" the driver asked.

"We're kind of new to the country. Where do you reckon we should live?"

He turned and looked at us with a beaming smile. "Not more bloody Poms. Why don't you try Ningaloo." It was time to buy a map of Australia!

The cool weather prompted us to keep moving and after exploring Melbourne, Tasmania and Adelaide, we contacted Jo and John and hopped on a train to Western Australia to meet them. It took three days and three nights to travel across the arid interior, including the Nullarbor, along the longest straight section of rail track in the world. The abundance of free time and the vast open spaces viewed from the carriage window gave us the chance to rest and assess our situation. I sensed that our travels were nearly over and the taxi driver's recommendation of visiting Ningaloo would have to wait.

We were fatigued from so many months and felt a surge of relief, knowing that we would see a familiar face at the platform. As the train rolled into the city centre I stole a final glimpse at our travel map. We were at the western edge of the continent, in the most isolated city in the world and it was time to hang our walking boots up.

John looked very different to the man we had bumped into at the migration seminar in Sandown eighteen months earlier. The woollen coat, designer jeans and soft leather boots had been replaced by a bright blue Billabong T-shirt, retro shorts, and open-toed sandals. His mousey hair had been bleached by the sun and a designer pair of wrap-around sunglasses hid his eyes. He drove us along the coast road towards his home, pointing out various landmarks as his four-wheel drive rumbled past million-dollar properties overlooking the wide expanse of the Indian Ocean.

It was a strange feeling listening to John's hearty chuckles as he asked questions about our trip and then shared his experiences since moving from the UK. He was infatuated with the area and was keen to give us as much support as possible to get us started. It all seemed too good to be true. I gazed out of the car window and thought how life would be for us from now on. Every few seconds we passed joggers, dog walkers and bare-chested teenage boys holding surfboards, en route to the water. Across from the white sands the ocean twinkled sedately and a flotilla of sailboats stretched across the horizon. A few teenagers frolicked in the gentle surf and a family of sunbathers were stretched out on colourful beach towels, but in all essence the beach was empty.

I turned to face John and asked, "Where is everyone? The beaches are empty and it's the weekend." He had been waiting for the question and replied, "It's April, so this is early autumn. Those sunbathing are probably holidaymakers or newly-arrived migrants. It's too cold for most Aussies now."

As he drove along the coast road I checked the digital reading displayed on the car console. 29 degrees. I glanced at the number again and had a sudden flashback to a day trip at Margate Beach a decade earlier. During the car journey, BBC Radio 2 excitedly announced that the "heatwave across southern England was the hottest in a decade with temperatures approaching 30 degrees." I arrived in Margate to find that the overflow carparks were filled with inflamed drivers and upon reaching the beach, gazed upon a plethora of white-fleshed families crammed onto the golden sands, segregated by colourful windbreaks and discarded plastic buckets. Sunburnt kids queued impatiently for ice creams, and dehydrated donkeys trudged along the sea front, oblivious to the shrieks of laughter from those that braved the tepid waters. Despite all this, it had been a memorable day trip and it suddenly dawned on me that those simple English seaside occasions were now resigned to history if this was to be our new home.

I made a mental note to ask John what type of holidays the citizens of Perth went on. It seemed that this was idyllic, but would pristine beaches and blue skies become monotonous after awhile?

As John drove I closed my eyes and tried to think through all the things that now needed consideration. Finding work, looking for a place to live and hoping that we would be able to make a go of life in this faraway place. I must have nodded off, as the next thing I heard was high-pitched giggling and someone knocking on the passenger window. We had arrived at John and Jo's house and their two young girls were keen to say hello.

Would we ever have made it to Perth if we hadn't stopped for a muffin and coffee during the interval at the migration seminar? Whether it was fate, destiny or just good luck, I don't know. But as Jo showed us to our room and then led us to the outdoor pool I felt as though we were in some type of dream. We had arrived in Australia with a rucksack each and were now living rent-free in a detached house near the Indian Ocean. I was down to my last pair of shorts, hadn't worked for a year and was now in a position to restart my career. I sat by the edge of the pool, dangled my legs into the clear warm water and turned my face towards the setting sun.

The nearest country was four hour's flight away, the nearest city was three days drive away, my best mate Steve was 10,000 km away and our family fully expected us to return home within a few years. We were finally in Australia after years of dreaming, but I felt excited and scared at the same time. Excited about the future but scared of letting go of the past. No one in Western Australia knew that I enjoyed walking in the Lake District and had once cycled from Land's End to John O'Groats using my brother's bike because I couldn't afford my own. In an area the size of Russia I had no history.

As days turned to weeks, the utopia ended with the realisation that I was no longer travelling but was now living in a city far from my hometown. It was the simple things that I missed. Bumping into a friend at the shops, going out for beers on a Friday night or dropping round for a cuppa with my sister, Alice. It was clear no amount of sunset walks on the nearby beach at Sorrento could suppress my sentimental memories of life back in England.

I needed two things: a job and a purpose. My CV had

been emailed to the HR desks of every manufacturing organisation in Perth and all I could do was wait for the phone to ring. My purpose came unexpectedly one hazy afternoon when John asked me to help him collect a second-hand boat that he had purchased on the weekend. The conversation went something like this...

"I didn't know you liked boats, John?"

"I'm not sure if I do, but we're in Australia now and you gotta live the dream. That's why we're here, isn't it?"

I smiled at his reply and asked, "What type did you buy?"

He grinned and answered simply, "A blue and white one." I looked at him quizzically, "Do you know how to steer one?" John chuckled and replied, "No, but it can't be that hard."

Four hours later, Sea Eagle was parked in his driveway. It was eight metres long, painted blue and white, with twin engines and below-deck seating. We didn't know how to start the engine or untie the anchor and were baffled by the amount of worn ropes stowed in the hold. While Jo and their children clambered aboard in a fit of giggles and excited laughter, John searched for the ignition switch and called out loud with each new discovery.

That weekend he enrolled in an accelerated skippers course to learn all about boats, which culminated in a successful man overboard simulation in Hillarys boat harbour. While John studied boating regulations, I purchased two rods, a fishing magazine, an assortment of hooks, a packet of bait and a large plastic bucket. After two days training, the instructor deemed him competent to captain the Sea Eagle and that evening by his pool we made plans for the launch.

The TV weatherman warned that the hot weather was refusing to budge and it would be another scorcher, so we decided to drive to the marina just before sunrise. This would be good for multiple reasons: There would be no one around to watch us get it wrong if our inaugural attempt failed and we would be back on land before getting sunburnt.

Sea Eagle

The access road to the marina was whisper-quiet as we turned into the carpark the next morning. Each wide bay was specifically designed for boat trailers and four-wheel drives and boldly segregated with fresh white paint. As John reversed the boat onto the ramp, the sun threatened to appear on the horizon and under a waking sky the Sea Eagle slid easily into the glassy water.

John effortlessly steered through the marina, past million-dollar yachts clinking sedately in the fresh breeze and made his way past the small unmanned lighthouse and into the Indian Ocean. According to my fishing magazine, the reefs that skirt the marina were teeming with fish so we chose the nearest rocks, threw the anchor overboard and prepared our gear. In between nibbles one of us would jump overboard to cleanse early morning sweat from our eyes and then dive below the surface to search for missing fish.

We were close enough to the beach to watch early morning dog walkers stroll along the shoreline and as the wind picked up, excited barks carried over the azure water. The early ambience changed as the sun climbed steadily and although still relatively low on the horizon, I could feel the rising heat on my exposed scalp.

With an empty bait packet and an unused bucket we upped anchor and returned to the boat ramp, where Fran and Jo were waiting to greet us. As we entered the marina, the faint smell of diesel competed with the wisp of grilled bacon, as moored residents prepared for a day on the water.

On the main jetty, an excited throng of people waited in line to board the fast ferry that would take them across to the nearby island of Rottnest. With no cars allowed on the island, many passengers had hired bicycles and as we glided past, the ferry workers loaded them carefully onto the bow. In an hour's time the marina would be a hive of activity, with locals, tourists, fishermen, kayakers, swimmers and coffee addicts embracing the sunshine.

But as we approached shore, it was clear that the boat ramp was no longer empty. With military precision, we watched as two vessels were launched in quick succession, their owners making the task look simple. We waited for a gap and came alongside the ramp and within minutes were ready to winch the boat out of the water, and while John steadied the sides I jumped overboard to collect the car and trailer.

It was all going well, including my first-ever attempt at reversing a trailer down the boat ramp, and we were on track for soon enjoying a coffee by the foreshore. John connected the bow to the steel cable of the trailer and waded into the water to line up the keel. As he steadied the stern, I pushed the button to initiate the electric motor, but the wiring had shorted and we were met by silence. I repeatedly tried the button and wiggled the wire, but there was no sign of life from the motor. The only option left was to use the manual winch. I located the handle, slotted it into position and began to turn. The steel cable squeaked in protest, but the Sea Eagle rocked gently as it edged from the water. I increased my speed and for a few seconds it slid towards the trailer. Just as the bow edged towards the first roller, the winch arm snapped, revealing a wide vein of rust as the broken piece fell to the floor.

For a few seconds we stared at the sheared metal and contemplated our next move. Jo ran over and assessed the situation, looking back and forth from the car to the water's edge. "I've got an idea," she announced confidently. "We can tie a rope directly from the bow to the tow bar of the car. All we need to do is chock the trailer and pull the boat into place. Easy!"

John returned to the water to steady the stern one more while I went in search of the rope. The trailer wheels were chocked using fragments of discarded paving slabs and Jo gave me the thumbs up that all knots on the rope were tight. All I had to do was pull the Sea Eagle out of the water so that it slid onto the top of the trailer and as I started the engine I waited for the signal from John.

The first power walkers of the day were now in transit and a few stopped to watch our predicament. I was hoping they would move away, but maybe they knew something we didn't. They waited patiently while John rechecked all knots and realigned the drifting vessel. I was temporarily distracted by an Oasis track humming from the car stereo and as the rising sun warmed my face I gently tapped my fingers on the steering wheel. It had been a magical morning and a world away from the TV reports of blizzards in the UK.

John yelled out, "Go Ali." and on his command I pushed the accelerator just as Liam Gallagher belted out, "Don't Look Back in Anger." As I skidded up the wet ramp the next voice I heard from the waterfront was Fran's. It was shrilled and sounded very urgent but the music was too loud to make out all her words.

A freak gust had pulled the stern off centre at the instant that John had given me the command. Oblivious to this fact, I had continued up the ramp, towing the skewed boat behind me. It failed to line up with the centre of the chocked trailer and wedged itself at an obscure angle into the side, just as I heard Fran's cries to stop.

While contemplating a hasty reversal to ease the tension on the rope, a four-wheel drive vehicle motored past, towing a white fibreglass twin-engine boat with the words *Wave Dancer* scrolled on the side. The driver and passengers were all wearing wrap-around sunglasses and turned their heads towards me as they hunted for the nearest parking spot.

They would soon be ready to launch and by now I understood the process. Drive in, walk down to the ramp, check it was clear, reverse the trailer into the water, unhitch the boat, and drive off the ramp. Then park the car, board the vessel and head offshore in search of fish. I sensed we had overstayed our welcome and this was confirmed when another vehicle drove past, this time pulling a small aluminium dinghy. I scanned the main road and saw two dinghies being towed towards the marina. I felt beads of moisture on my neck and wondered if it was anxiety or early morning sweat. Back home in England I would just be getting out of bed at this time. But temperature can dictate behaviour and it was clear that in Australia, those that enjoy water sports were used to quick breakfasts.

I reached over and turned off the music. It suddenly seemed very quiet, except for a pair of seagulls arguing over a discarded croissant. I left the engine running and ran along the edge of the carpark then down the boat ramp and realised that nothing had gone to plan. The quayside was dotted with bystanders and impatient boaties who stood on the finger jetty with their arms folded. They were all staring at Sea Eagle, which was on its side, halfway up the ramp with its bow wedged into the side of the buckled trailer.

Fran was standing nearby, her arms held wide and Jo was calling something out to me, but I couldn't take my eyes off the carnage. John was still in the water and his voice bellowed across the marina, "Ali, I couldn't help it. The wind picked up and moved the boat. We shouted for you to stop pulling. Didn't you hear?"

Before I could reply I heard a mumbled comment from a man standing on the finger jetty and turned to face him. My face felt flushed and I smiled, hoping to make light of the situation.

"Did you say something, mate?"

"Yes, I did. Bloody useless Poms!"

He was right of course, on both accounts. We were useless and we were Poms. But we were beginners at boating and I had always thought Australians gave everyone a fair go. Now I realised this didn't extend to bailing out clueless migrants on one of the busiest mornings in weeks. I felt like replying with a witty remark. After all, that's what the English are known for in moments of crisis, but Fran sensed my mood and called out, "I hope you're asking him for help."

Maybe we would have sorted out the problem, but time was not on our side and it was clear we needed urgent assistance. There was a growing backlog of boats waiting to launch and a small flotilla was now waiting in the marina, eager to get home with their catch of the day. This was an Australian traffic jam and we were in danger of causing boat ramp rage. John walked out of the water, took one look at the trailer and then scanned the crowd for a friendly face. After less than six months in the country he was a natural at connecting with Australians. Maybe it was the bleached hair, olive complexion and easygoing manner.

He held his arms wide in a gesture of submission and called out, "Does anyone know what to do next?"

A booming voice echoed across the marina as one of the onlookers replied, "Yes. Go back to Pommy Land, mate, or take up table tennis."

John smiled at the remark and appealed for help once more. This time there was a different reaction. One of the bystanders unfolded his arms and tapped a friend on the shoulder to help. They ambled over, inspected the situation with an assured look and within minutes had the vessel back in the water and lined up squarely. One of them requested my keys, reversed the car and expertly dragged the Sea Eagle from the water onto the buckled trailer. Within fifteen minutes all was calm. The boaties were on the water, the walkers were striding along the ocean view pathway and we were in a coffee shop discussing our first fishing expedition in Australia.

From that day on, Sea Eagle gave us plenty of opportunities for adventure. On good days the engine would behave and as we skimmed along the flat ocean, dolphins would leap from the water, then surf in our wake. On rare occasions we even managed to pluck a few fish from the deep.

But minor incidents kept occurring. During the course of a month, we became stuck on sandbanks, suffered engine failure multiple times and even had to be towed back to the marina by Sea Rescue. Our energy waned and other commitments took over our lives.

In the true spirit of entrepreneurs, Jo and John were looking at the multitude of opportunities that abound in this faraway place and Sea Eagle slowly lost her appeal. It was also time for Fran and me to find our own place to call home. While we searched the weekend papers for accommodation, John suggested a farewell, for Sea Eagle and us.

Our final trip was crossing a section of the Indian Ocean towards Perth's favourite playground, Rottnest Island. Amateur skippers who don't know how to navigate the deep stretch sometimes follow the tourist ferry as it makes its way across the choppy waters. But the waters around Perth are notorious for treacherous reefs and although we were naive, we were not totally insane.

We hired a local skipper who steered us safely towards the low-lying island within two hours. The sky was a perfect blue, with just a hint of wind to stir up the ocean, and Sea Eagle ploughed easily through the white horses as dolphins frolicked in our bow. As Rottnest Island came into view, the water changed colour. Unlike the monotone sky, the sparkling waters of the bay were a fusion of blues and greens and as I threw the anchor overboard, my eyes were drawn to the abundance of fish swimming in the deep pools of warm water.

During our celebratory breakfast at an ocean view café, John announced an end to his ocean-faring days and on our return to the mainland Sea Eagle was put up for sale. It was purchased a few weeks later, to a seasoned Australian who knew how to catch fish. We were eager to make changes too. Our *sliding door* moment was over and it was time for us to make our own way in Australia.

5

MUSHROOMS

"Home is not a place, it's a feeling."
Unknown

Apr 22nd 1889. The Oklahoma land rush begins.
Apr 22nd 2003. We go shopping for mushrooms.

We had been living in Australia a few months and finally had secure jobs. Our rucksacks were gathering dust, hanging from hooks in the garage of our rented unit and weekends were spent relaxing on the nearby beach at Sorrento. Balmy evenings promised by the presenters at the migration seminar were just as they promised, and we began to embrace outdoor living in our cosy backyard. It seemed that the hype had been true and at last we were living the great Australian dream. But the wakeup call came one Saturday morning during a late breakfast. As I munched on my raisin toast I called out to Fran, "Have you seen the headlines? Perth house prices poised to soar."

She stood alongside me and we studied neat little graphs depicting the latest hotspot suburbs and predicted trends as the Perth property market awoke from years of hibernation. But we were still on a high from backpacking and the last thing we wanted was a property boom. This was the third week running that the topic had made the front pages and it seemed to be the hottest news in town. For the next few weeks we soaked up the autumn sunshine and hoped the news would go away, but the media seemed infatuated with the topic. Maybe there was nothing else to report in Perth?

My previous delving into the property market was in the late 1980s, when I purchased a century-old two bedroom terrace house in my home town of Luton, thirty miles north of London. My timing was impeccable, as I just managed to purchase on the crest of the housing boom, and within three years the mortgage had trebled and the house price had halved.

Now, it seemed, we needed to act quickly as the headlines were predicting rapid growth. In 2003, one of our reasons for moving to Perth was the cheap property prices compared to other parts of Australia. Every new migrant we met seemed confident that they would be trading their semi-detached home and Vauxhall Astra for a detached house near the beach and a Toyota Land Cruiser. Perth was historically under-priced and the silky presentations in the UK told us so, but it seemed that those days were rapidly coming to an end.

Our initial quandary was whether to purchase a block of land or an established house. In Britain, vacant land is so rare that it seldom gets discussed as an option, but Perth was expanding rapidly and every week the papers were filled with advertisements for brand new developments, with exotic names like Eagles Landing, Stockman's Retreat and Ocean Gardens. Radio adverts for new land sales were broadcast by an English actress and her soft Midlands accent was heard across the sprawling suburbs, encouraging drivers to head north to become part of the new community. Site works were already under way for manicured parks, shopping centres, schools and playgrounds, all within easy reach of the Indian Ocean. It seemed too good to be true and it was time to investigate.

Land sale posters are a common sight

Fran took control the following Saturday as once again the headlines ruined our breakfast. She suggested we go out for a coffee, check out the land sales and then head to Wanneroo markets for mushrooms on the way home. We should have realised by now that similar conversations about land prices were occurring throughout the city, with mild panic gripping all those contemplating a house move.

We headed north under another clear blue sky until the freeway ended, forcing us inland onto Perth's newest dual carriageway, which eventually turned into a freshly laid single lane, as suburbia gave way to bushland. Flags, banners and giant advertising boards displaying pictures of smiling families playing on tranquil beaches lined the final stretch of tarmac as we came to the temporary end of north Perth.

In the distance, rows of display homes overlooked a manmade lake and tucked at the end of a gravelled carpark we discovered a large portable cabin, with the words *Land Sale* brazenly displayed across the front.

The parking bays were full despite the early hour and inside the cabin excited couples mulled over colourful leaflets, land plans and a papier-mâché layout that stood centre stage in an attempt to visualise the land developer's vision. I could feel the air of anticipation as potential buyers whispered to their partners and scanned the leaflets for information. While Fran went in search of a pamphlet I studied the buyers. Most were under forty and many of the men proudly wore their sporting colours. Now I understood where all the Brits were moving to in Perth.

In the foyer a colourful poster read, "Stage 9 selling fast. Stage 10 land release in three months." I turned to Fran and whispered, "Forget the coffee and mushrooms. We need to buy some land today."

Her eyes widened, "Ali, we need to think about this."

But I was caught in the moment and persisted. "Read that poster and look at the way people are behaving. This is the 1889 Oklahoma Land Rush all over again and I'm not waiting until the only available land is parched savannah deep in Indian country."

She looked at me quizzically and asked, "What are you on about? Have you drunk enough water this morning?"

I pointed to the entrance. "Look at the faces of that couple by the door. Their eyes bulged as soon as they walked in and saw the number of people inside. Everybody here today is intent on buying, not window-shopping. They're all spooked. I'm telling you, by this afternoon these blocks will be gone and the next stage will rise by 20%, if not more."

Fran's eyes widened and she asked, "Since when have you been a property expert?"

"Never, and guess what, my track record shows that

I've only ever bought at the peak. If we buy today, for once in my life I will be ahead!"

She smiled softly and replied, "You're acting very dramatic, but let's have a look."

I stood by a couple that were studying the papier-mâché model, then referring back to the land prices on a printout. They were in their mid-twenties and by their distinct accent, were born and bred Australians. I heard him whisper to his wife, "Block 201 is perfect. It's got a north facing back garden where the pool can go and we can fit an alfresco on the west side to catch the sea breezes." I discreetly moved away and pulled Fran to one side. "Block 201 is about to go. It's all about having your back garden facing north for the pool and thinking about westerly breezes. You join the queue and I'll look for another like it." She was third in line to put her name down. Each person took just one minute to fill in the simple form and then handed over a thousand dollars deposit for first refusal.

By my estimation, I had three minutes to locate our dream block. The couple after 201 were now at the counter, so I scanned the available blocks and found that 202 looked favourable. *We could be their neighbours*, I thought, and glanced at them while they filled out their forms. They were casually dressed, wearing board shorts and matching blue and yellow t-shirts emblazoned with the words, *West Coast Eagles Football Club*. Maybe they would let us use their pool and we could enjoy cold beers together on their alfresco and discuss the technicalities of Australian Football, known throughout most of the country as *The Footy*.

With the numbers 202 scribbled on my hand, I made my way towards Fran but midstride, the sales representative on the front desk called out, "Please be aware that blocks 201, 209 and 202 are now on hold."

Well, there went the new neighbours and the chance to learn about the footy! Fran was near the front of the queue and looked back quizzically as I stood motionless adjacent to the queue. I turned quickly, my heart racing as the adrenalin pumped. It was now a game and I dare not lose.

While deciding between a 678 m2 corner block with an eastern-facing garden and a 400 m2 block near the ocean, I heard my name echo through the confined cabin. Fran was at the front desk and eager for help!

I took one more look, made a once-in-a-lifetime decision, memorised the number of the chosen block, and then ran past the growing queue of hopefuls towards the front. A few moments later we put our names down for a corner block with an east facing back garden.

"Great choice," cooed the sales rep. "I've always loved block 214."

A woman behind us let out a loud tut, unable to hide the fact that she was planning to purchase the same block. She peeled away from the queue, noisily talking into her phone while stomping back to the papier-mâché model. The customer rep handed over a glossy map of the new sub divisions and circled our block in red ink to help us locate it. We walked past the growing queue and with a mixed feeling of excitement and trepidation, stepped outside into bright sunshine, in search of a wooden peg somewhere in the streets with no names.

Once clear of the gravelled carpark and colourful flags it was obvious that there was little in the way of infrastructure. The whole area was morphing from vision into reality and most natural bush that had once thrived had been stripped bare. The result was a featureless terrain of yellow sand interwoven with freshly laid tarmac roads. The developers, it seemed, went in for the shock and awe tactic of levelling the land to make for easy building. A few patches of bush still remained and were being converted into parks and we discovered a large artificial lake strategically located a few kilometres inland. The blocks around the water were artistically named as cottage blocks, with little room left for a back garden once the house was built, but water views were a demand item and they had all sold.

After a quick scout of the area, we found a wooden peg marked 214 and parked on the vacant block. The surrounding land was devoid of completed houses, but numerous sold signs meant that this was soon to change. According to the map, our block was about a kilometre from the Indian Ocean and I suddenly felt excited at the prospect of an ocean view. I called out to Fran, "Get on my shoulders, you might be able to see the water," and held onto the retaining wall as she clambered on. As I steadied myself, her excited voice called out. "Oh, yes, I can see waves. We'll have ocean views if we build a double storey."

She jumped down onto the coarse sand and I studied the map once again. At this moment in time she was right. But between our block and the beach were ten rows of unbuilt streets. Each row nearer to the beach increased incrementally in cost and we couldn't afford to get any closer to the ocean. Now I could see why many residents chose to live by the manicured lake. The homes on the coast were going to be million-dollar properties and many would be double storey due to the small size of the block. With ten houses in front of us, there was no way of gaining an ocean view as the terrain was too flat.

We sat on the warm sand, finished the last of our water and waited for the westerly breeze to cool us down. With only a few established houses in the vicinity, we could see far across the vacant blocks and watched as the new owners of block 201 measured their backyard. The guy was taking giant steps along the sand, probably checking where their pool would go.

It was then that I had a thought. "Fran, what can you hear?"

She looked across at me, "Nothing much, just a bulldozer and that guy calling numbers out to his wife."

"Can you hear the waves?"

"Just about."

"Anything else?"

She turned and looked at me, "What are you on about?"

"There are no sounds of wildlife. No birds singing, no kangaroos skipping, no parrots squawking. Just hundreds of ants marching across the sand and they don't make a sound."

We looked towards the clear blue sky and watched rose-breasted cockatoos fly overhead, but none stopped to rest. Why would they? There was nothing to eat and nowhere to roost. I understood that the development would eventually become established and the new homeowners would lay manicured lawns with neat borders. Many residents would introduce vegetable plots and plant seedlings, but trees would take years to grow tall. Somehow, the exuberance of purchasing our own land and finding a master builder to create a dream home didn't seem appealing anymore. I remembered back to my wedding speech when our dreams were about living in the country, having free-range chickens and maybe even a Vietnamese potbellied pig. The nearest chicken to this block would be Kentucky fried in the new fast food takeaway being built in the master planned shopping centre.

Maybe Fran could read my mind. She turned to me and suggested, "Why don't we try an established house? Somewhere with a few trees and a big back garden." It was clear that the Oklahoma Land Rush was not meant to be for us, although it had been an eventful morning. As we went in search of mushrooms, Fran waved to the man at block 201 but he was too busy pacing out his west-facing alfresco to look up.

A few months later I strolled to our local deli to collect the Saturday paper. The sun was still warm despite the fact that it was officially winter and a flock of noisy parrots nestled in nearby peppermint trees. Back at home I sat on the veranda of our twenty year-old-property and read the front page while Fran made tea and toasted the last of the raisin bread. She stood over my shoulder as I read the headline, *Campers Queue for Weeks for Next Land Release as Prices Rise by 20%*. I thought back to the couple that purchased block 201 and hoped their pool and alfresco would come to fruition.

We had opted to buy a house in an established suburb and were pleased to find that our neighbourhood contained a cosmopolitan mix. The majority were Australians (both white and indigenous), with a compliment of Europeans, South Africans and Asians. The lawns in our street were well kept, the ocean was only a five-minute drive away and the local children were mischievous but polite. Fran was blooming in the early stages of pregnancy and we had found our first Australian home.

6

A JOB FOR LIFE

"The only way to do great work is to love what you do."
Steve Jobs

2004. Perth, Western Australia.

My dad had one simple piece of advice for his children: "The most important thing when you leave school is to get a trade. It'll get you a job for life." He was born near the shipyards of Port Glasgow in Scotland and as a teenager moved to England in search of work. Luton was a thriving industrial town and it was here that he learnt his engineering trade.

Years later, I followed his advice and took a position as an electrician in one of the largest manufacturing organisations in the country. At its peak, Vauxhall Motors employed 20,000 people and inside the sprawling factory it resembled a small town. There was a 24-hour canteen, lunch hour hairdressers, a fully stocked bar and even a snooker hall.

Throughout my years at Vauxhall I constantly bumped into Dad's friends and embraced the handshakes, pats on the back and encouragement. It was apparent that he was a well-known and respected man. It took me many years to carve my own identity and during this period Vauxhall Motors realised that my real skills lay beyond screwdrivers and voltage testers. My last four years at the car plant were spent wearing a shirt and tie, surrounded by colleagues discussing future plans for automated machinery and improvement opportunities.

When I enrolled for University studies to assist with my career change I assured Dad that my electrical skills would never be forgotten. The importance of having a trade became apparent when, without warning, Vauxhall announced the closure of its car manufacturing operations, sending shockwaves through the community as the news of redundancies and job losses gripped the town. Throughout the emotional unrest, union marches and political interaction, it was clear that the factory was doomed. For a new life away from the country, it was my city and guilds qualifications that proved the vital difference. They were the essential item that Australia requested, in order to grant a skilled migration visa.

But no matter how gifted you are and despite your technical feats of accomplishment in other parts of the world, the Australian Government will not recognise your technical skills until a trained assessor proves you competent. After a few months living in Australia it felt time to gain the required certificate, without which I was unable to work as a licensed electrician. I signed up for an evening course at the local technical college, and attended every Tuesday for the next six months.

I can still recall the first moments of our inaugural lesson. It was a warm summer's evening and the room was filled with experienced electricians recently arrived from all corners of the globe and most were eager to kickstart their careers in the land of opportunity. The lecturer, a quietly spoken South African, introduced himself and handed out a workbook called *Electrical Fundamentals*. The subject of the first lesson was called *The Atom*. In fairness, since completing my apprenticeship I had often overlooked the vital role of electrons and protons, and maybe the Australian Government was suspicious that all new migrants also ignored this crucial element of electrical theory.

As the workbooks were passed around, there was stunned silence as the mature students scanned the contents of their handouts. A few minutes earlier they had met in the foyer for the first time, with tentative conversations during the walk to the classroom. But even these brief chats revealed a vast array of electrical experience and technical knowledge. I estimated that the average age of the students was mid-thirties, giving each person about fifteen years post apprenticeship experience. As our lecturer drew a picture of an atom on the whiteboard, the guy sharing my table, a blonde-haired, potbellied Londoner, called out, "This is ridiculous, mate. I've been a house sparky for twelve years and why do I need to learn about atoms now?"

Before the lecturer could answer, a barrage of other questions reverberated throughout the classroom.

"Are you telling me that I've just given up an electrical business in Johannesburg to sit here and listen about the atom?"

"Look, pal, I've been an electrical contractor in Glasgow for ten years and just want to start my own business. Why do I need to learn about the atom?"

The wave of discontent continued as the classmates shared their electrical skills, business experience and opinions of the atom with each other. The lecturer smiled throughout and when silence once again descended, he walked into the middle of the room and gave the best advice of the semester.

"Guys, just get over it. You're here every Tuesday for the next six months and can either fight the system or use the time to relearn some electrical basics. While on campus it's an ideal time to form professional relationships with each other and a year from now some of you may be in business together."

He was absolutely right. During the months ahead, some constantly complained, always comparing electrical standards in Australia with those from their countries of origin. The reply was always the same. "You're in Australia now, so follow our regulations or change careers." Most calmed down and although they didn't always admit it, I sensed that everyone in the classroom benefited from the compulsory refresher in some way during the six-month period.

Within weeks of being certified to wire an Australian three-phase motor I found myself working as a contract shift electrician for a national brickmaking manufacturer. Part way through my second week I realised that Vauxhall Motors had trained me extremely well, both as an electrician and as a Production Engineer. I was conditioned to working within a global organisation that had stringent processes, systems and procedures, but working in the brick factory was like stepping back thirty years.

For my role as a shift electrician I had to wear a fluorescent orange boiler suit, yellow hard hat, protective glasses and steel toe-capped boots. At least they seemed to take safety seriously. I reported to an elusive maintenance manager who rarely visited the electricians except to hand out jobs each morning and to call us whenever a new breakdown had occurred. Life consisted of mediocre electrical installation jobs, then abandoning them to race to breakdowns on old machinery that had rarely been maintained. The disgruntled electricians sat for tea each break time, reading week-old papers, moaning about the management, and clock-watching until home time.

This wasn't living the dream as portrayed in the glossy presentations in the seminars and as I trundled through the dusty factory I yearned to use my skills in productivity improvement. My breakthrough came after another long breakdown, which once again became a farcical run-around as electricians, engineers and supervisors blundered through another crisis. As calm prevailed once more, I walked into the maintenance office, found a marker pen and drew a large fishbone diagram on the whiteboard. I will never forget the conversation from the manager as he walked in and saw me scribbling.

"Alistair, what are you doing?"

"I'm trying to help if that's ok? Did you know that the same fault occurred last week and a few months earlier? All the production operators are talking about it as the downtime was hours. Have you thought about getting all the stakeholders together for a problem-solving-session?"

He walked towards his computer and replied sharply, "Don't get too concerned. That's my business and what's that you're drawing?"

"It's a fishbone diagram that can help us work out what went wrong over the last twelve hours."

"Whatever do I want one of them for?" he snorted loudly.

"It's a production improvement tool used to get to the root cause of the problem."

"Listen to me, Alistair. We don't need that type of thing here and you're just an electrical contractor who's getting a bit carried away."

I forced myself to remain calm, took a deep breath and answered, "I reckon the maintenance team does need to improve. I may only be a contractor, but I feel part of the team. We're just repeating the same mistakes over and over again. As for being a sparky, have you ever looked at my CV? I'm keen to help, as the team are constantly frustrated with the same problems and surely it must drive you crazy as well?"

"Look Alistair, they always complain. That's what workers do. You leave the management side to me and get back to the maintenance workshop where you belong."

While driving home that evening I knew there was work to do, as it was clear that my skills from the UK were being underutilised. Maybe it was isolation from the rest of the world or just ignorance, but if this was a typical Australian manufacturer then I was capable of making a real change. Being categorised as a shift electrician was part of the problem. I rewrote my CV, targeted organisations that strove for continuous improvement and soon found myself managing a production team of 180 people for a caravan manufacturer.

The moral of this story is simple. If you were a team leader in your home country, then consider yourself a supervisor by the time you touch down in Australia. If you were a supervisor, then stretch yourself and look at management positions. If you were a competent maintenance tradesman, the chances are that you already know a lot about systems, procedures and how to maintain and manage them. You just may not realise it.

In my experience, migrants from Europe, South Africa and Asia have been trained well and are familiar with vigorous procedures and high accountability. If you sell these skills and attributes and believe in yourself then you should be able to move up a step as you find work in Australia.

I never went back to electrical work. I realised that my skills and passion lay in the world of productivity and business improvement. Two years later, I gained a Six Sigma black belt in Business Improvement, then studied the art of facilitation and gained employment for one of the largest mining companies in Australia.

7

A NEW AUSTRALIAN

"Every child is an artist. The problem is how to remain an artist once we grow up."
Pablo Picasso

2004. Perth, Western Australia.

Fran was preparing to have a baby and I was out of my comfort zone. Our new life revolved around birth plans, pregnancy yoga, and antenatal classes. If we had been living in England, family and friends would have helped steer us through the minefield of emotions and changes that occur when a new baby is about to enter the world. But apart from a few newfound friends, we were still mostly alone.

My sister, Alice, sensed our need and touched down in Australia two months before the due date. She waltzed through customs like she had just been on a bus ride to town, not an arduous flight from England. Her fair hair was hidden under a summer bonnet, but her smile was a sight to behold.

Alice
Wild water breaks over our raft
As the Zambezi roars
On our global adventure
Now a lifetime away
We once lived as nomads
From the Amazon to the Andes
And Kilimanjaro to Cape Town
When we land on Australia's distant shores
You whisper
I'm pregnant
But we have no close friends
This side of the equator
And you have so many questions
About birth plans, yoga, and vitamins
Which I know so little about
But then a call comes
From England, and everything will be fine
Alice, my sister, will be the cavalry
Mary Poppins, I think, as she waltzes through customs
Dressed for action, with backpack bursting
With gifts, goodies and womanly things
That I know nothing about
Under crimson skies, you walk barefoot
Like sisters
Along lonely beaches
One talks, another listens
Advice, gentle laughs, and constant reassurance
Each evening Alice shares stories
About being a mum

We laugh, until tears fall
Three weeks pass and it is time
For her departure
Alice hands us a gift
Steve Martin is funny in Parenthood, she says
And then she is gone
At 30,000 feet
London bound
Replaced so quickly
By Fran's mum and dad
Retired, excited, and eager to help
Fran's belly swells, prompting wild stares
From strangers
It won't be long now
Too many sleepless nights
Steve Martin was funny, as Alice predicted
We were laughing out loud
When Fran's waters broke
I froze the film and searched frantically
For the overnight bag
While Fran stayed calm
And followed the birth plan
Created weeks before, with Alice
Noah James came into our world,
A day later
A new Australian, born to migrants
The house was empty when I returned
From the maternity ward
And saw the TV still on
Steve Martin's flickering smile
Welcoming me to parenthood

8

WALKABOUT

Definition of Walkabout: A period of wandering as a nomad, often as undertaken by Aboriginal people who feel the need to leave the place where they are in contact with white society, and return for spiritual replenishment to their traditional way of life.
Macquarie Dictionary
2004. Kalgoorlie, Western Australia.

I switched off the phone and called out to Fran, "We need to get the spare room ready again." From out in the kitchen I heard her chuckle and she came swiftly into the study, her eyes wide with intrigue.

"Who is it this time?"

"Alan and Sam are coming for Christmas. And Blake, of course."

Fran smiled and replied eagerly, "We'd better finish off the pool decking and get the bar fridge stacked up."

Getting visitors from England was becoming a common trend each summer, as family and friends escaped the cold and rain in the UK and chose to celebrate Christmas on the beach. Alan and Sam were good friends and their son Blake was already looking forward to a planned trip to Rottnest Island. I had worked with Alan for many years at Vauxhall Motors in Luton, until the day the factory gates closed forever and by all accounts he had flourished since redundancy. No longer shackled by the monotony of shift work and the same machines to maintain, he had embraced the change, become self-employed and was reaping the rewards for all his hard work.

A decade earlier, we had lived under the same roof. Alan was the landlord and I was his friend and lodger. Those lager-fuelled bachelor days were now distant memories, but Sam loved Alan's adventurous streak and their relationship flourished from the first moment they met in Gretna Green, Scotland.

Just before our telephone conversation finished, Alan confirmed that his spirit of adventure remained strong. "Ali, do you reckon you could sort out a few days for a bit of a road trip. Just you and me. You know, something different. Maybe see a bit of the real Australia. What do you think?" I was eager to please and replied quickly, "Sounds like a challenge. I'll get back to you soon."

As I put down the phone, I thought back to his comment. The "real Australia." It seemed to me that the *real* Australia was in fact, a mystical side creatively described in travel brochures and promotional websites. There were no kangaroos bouncing down our street and Aboriginals only seemed to play the didgeridoo in shopping malls and Sunday markets.

That evening I lazed by the pool and while reading the weekend newspaper, one particular article caught my eye. It was about an historic event in 1952 when Perth was so sparsely populated that residents had to turn their lights on so that John Glenn, the first American to orbit earth, could locate the city during his historic space flight.

I dropped the paper, turned off the outside lamp and stared towards space. Perth had grown rapidly since that pivotal space flight and despite the ambient light of night-time suburbia, I could just make out the faint swirl of a million stars flickering above the most isolated city in the world. I suddenly felt very alone and far away from family. I closed my eyes and thought once more of England and those lazy summer days of 1976, with Mum sitting on the front porch while I played football in the street with friends.

Since moving to Australia, each call from family and friends triggered another yearning to return. Although it was wrong to do so, I kept comparing Australia with England and on each occasion the result was the same. They are poles apart. Conversations I had with other migrants from the UK often went something like this:

"Do you miss England?"

"No way. All that traffic and rain and grey skies."

"What about the English countryside?"

"What about it. I live near the beach now and I've got a pool as well."

"What about culture and diversity?"

"There is culture and diversity here but you need to search for it. The Australian lifestyle is laid-back. If you want more than that, take a holiday to Asia. Or move to Fremantle. If that's not quirky enough, then try Melbourne or Sydney! Look at it this way. My kids have freedom, the beaches are amazing, and long hot summers are guaranteed in Perth."

During numerous social occasions, I would seek out those who had settled from overseas and the questions were answered in a similar way each time. Maybe it was just me. I still missed the grittiness and bustle of London, the rolling hills and steep crags of the Lake District, the historic theatres of Covent Garden and the fact that I could get a train from St Pancras in the morning and arrive in Paris for lunch. Not that I had ever taken the channel tunnel for a Parisian lunch. It was just the fact that I could.

There was only one direction out of Western Australia by train. That was on the Indian Pacific, heading east across the vast interior, where it reached Sydney after four days. It seemed to me that most residents of Perth, established and newly arrived, were happy with their isolation as long as the sun was shining. Pristine beaches, remote surf breaks, fresh coffee, hot summers, traffic lights, traffic jams, fast food, new shopping malls, and sprawling suburbs, was the Australia I kept bumping into.

Since our global travels a few years earlier I still craved flea markets, the smell of spices on the trade winds and colourful characters from faraway places. Even the Australians I had met since landing in Perth seemed tame. Not that I expected Crocodile Dundee to serve me coffee at the local café each weekend, but where were all the characters promised in the brochures? The outer suburbs were filling with migrants, many from the UK, Asia and South Africa and finding a cosy pub was proving harder than I expected. There would be iconic pubs in Perth, maybe in the back streets of Fremantle or in the city centre, but I was yet to discover them.

It was clear that Alan's phone call had woken me from a slumber. We had arrived in Australia a few years earlier as backpackers. My tattered rucksack had contained one pair of sandals, numerous faded T-shirts, three pairs of worn trousers and a diary that I planned to turn into an adventure travel story. During our gap year adventure we had been chased by rhinos, stalked by lions and had to run from danger whilst deep underground in a Bolivian mine. Now the only excitement seemed to be getting up early to avoid the morning rush hour.

While walking along the beach the following morning, Fran said, "When Alan comes over, just remember that he loves doing things that are unique to each location he visits. When you were cycling from Land's End to John O'Groats with him, didn't he insist on only eating and drinking local produce whenever possible?" Her question triggered an instantaneous recollection of travels with Alan. I thought back to an image of him in the Highlands of Scotland as he tasted a wee dram of locally distilled whiskey in each bar in Aviemore, then cycled 70 miles the following morning with a thumping headache. When on holiday with him in Donegal he switched to Guinness and oysters for the week and insisted on talking to every fisherman, sheep farmer and musician who came into my Uncle Peter's pub, the Corner House. Alan was a great man to have travelling with you. He embraced each location, craved local knowledge and didn't mind getting his hands dirty.

But what was uniquely Australian that would inspire him? Perth is not renowned for being an adventure capital and after listening to Fran's observations, I sensed the answer lay beyond the manicured lawns and new housing estates. That evening as I sat by the pool, I asked her, "Can you see the Southern Cross when you gaze at the stars?" She put down her wine and tilted her head back to stare into space. After a few seconds she declared, "No. It's too hard with all the city lights."

"Exactly." I agreed. "If Alan wants adventure, then I'll take him away from the city and into the bush. I'm going to track down an Aboriginal guide and we'll sleep under the stars each night." She looked over at me, sipped her wine and whispered, "There you go, I always knew you'd crack the problem."

With the plan taking shape, I felt the adrenalin rush once more as I contemplated a fresh adventure and over the next few days called tourist information centres throughout Australia to request names of local Aboriginal guides. One such call went like this:

"Alice Springs Information Centre, how may I help?"

"Hi, my name's Alistair and I'm after information on hiring a guide."

"I'm sorry but we don't have anything to hire. This is an information centre."

"No, I want to hire an Aboriginal guide. You know, to take me and a friend on walkabout.'

"Oh you mean the Aboriginal Explorer. I can book you on that."

"What's the Aboriginal Explorer?"

"It's very popular with overseas visitors. You are part of a fully escorted tour and are driven from Ayres Rock to the Olgas where you can see the sunrise. Then back at the information centre you watch Aboriginals dance and they also play the didgeridoo. The coach is air-conditioned and lunch is included."

It sounded like the bus would be filled with overweight Germans and snap-happy Japs. I contemplated Alan's muted reaction if I booked such a trip and hastily asked, "Is there anything, you know, more real. More authentic. This might sound funny, but I'm in search of the *real* Australia." I explained excitedly, "I don't want air-conditioned comfort. I want an Aboriginal guide to take me and my friend into the bush, to teach us to hunt and each evening we could camp under the stars in a swag and fall asleep while gazing at the Milky Way."

For a few seconds there was an awkward silence. Then she whispered, "I think I know what you mean, but we don't get many calls about that type of thing. Please hold and I'll ask around the office." She must have covered the earpiece with her hand, as all I could hear was a garbled message while she spoke with her colleagues. "This guy on the line... He's English, I think...Walkabout...Aboriginal...Not a pretend tour. But real one...Does anyone do this?...Not sure...Seems genuine...OK. I'll tell him." I heard her voice again, crisp and clear.

"Hello, thanks for holding. I know this sounds crazy but no one seems to do this anymore. I'm really sorry."

I could tell she was genuinely aggrieved but I couldn't hold back my frustration and asked, "Are you telling me that there is not one Aboriginal guide that can take me on a walkabout?"

"Well there might be plenty, but we rarely get calls for that type of request from visitors. Most people want a morning tour, followed by lunch and then they head back to their motels each evening. I can book you into one of them if you like and have availability for tomorrow but somehow I don't think it's for you and your friend."

I thanked the girl and hung up then tried putting the conversation into context. In Kenya, you can walk with

Massai across their pastoral lands, in Peru you can experience life in a remote jungle village but in Australia the only native activity I could find was watching tribal dances taking place in tourist information centres. I knew there would be much more on offer and began to delve deeper.

I typed "Adventure Australia" into Google and the screen filled with multiple options targeting those in search of guided bus trips to Ayers Rock, Fraser Island or The Great Barrier Reef. I was after somewhere more local and refined the search to "Adventure Western Australia Aborigine Guide."

The results were disappointing unless I chose a day trip from Perth to an area known as The Pinnacles. Numerous web pages informed me that they were once inhabited by Aboriginals and are part of the Nambung national park, just two hours north of Perth. The excursion is also famous for Billy Connolly running naked past the limestone formations during sunset. Although they were worthy of visiting, I felt that the Pinnacles wouldn't quench Alan's thirst for adventure, and continued to search.

Only the desperate keep scrolling through page after page on Google and by this stage, I fitted this category perfectly. It was on page 22 that I found a promising link. It took me to a basic web page that read, "Learn about Aboriginal people, Aboriginal culture, bush tucker and the Dreamtime." My hands were shaking as I hastily called the phone number on display. It answered on the eighth ring and the voice at the other end sounded deep and relaxed.

"Hello."

"Hi, my name is Alistair. I've just seen your article on

the web about bush tucker tours and would like to talk with Geoff..."

"Where do you want to go?"

"Are you Geoff?"

"Yes, of course I am. You just called my number. Where do you want to go?"

"I don't know really. My mate is coming over from England and we want an Aboriginal adventure and after lots of searching, I found your name on Google."

There was a moment of silence, and then Geoff replied, "When do you wanna come?"

"How about 18th December for three nights?"

"OK. Call me again when you arrive. It'll be getting hot by then, you know? I'll take you into the bush, no worries. Maybe we will talk about the Dreamtime and I'll show you how to find bush tucker. Does that sound ok?" I gripped the phone hard, the excitement rising in my voice. "That's great, Geoff. What about payment and where to meet?"

"What's your name again?"

"Alistair."

"I won't charge you much. Just call me when you arrive. Bring a swag, a knife and a torch and make sure you wear old clothes. What's your friend's name?"

"Alan"

"He's English hey, like you. He been to the bush before?"

"No, like I said..."

"Does he eat kangaroo?"

"Don't worry about Alan, he'll eat anything. Geoff, can I just confirm..." I was cut off as Geoff called out, "I gotta go. Call me when you arrive in Kal."

As I put down the phone, I felt the adrenalin rising. We

would be taking an excursion into what visitors call "The Outback" and Australians call "The Bush." This is their name for the wild landscape that epitomises the interior and describes all types of landscapes, from desert, swamp, savannah to scrubland. But more than anything, it defines the harsh red centre. It is a vast semi desert, typified by extremes, as searing daytime temperatures plunge quickly as soon as darkness descends.

At dusk the ancient landscape is bathed in a scorching red as the setting sun ignites the ochre embedded into the earth and rock, captivating all those that venture into the heartland. It is an unforgiving environment, sparsely populated by farmers, nomadic gold speculators and Aboriginal townships. Thriving communities do exist. Their wealth comes from deep underground and one of the most famous outback cities is Kalgoorlie in Western Australia.

Kalgoorlie owes its existence to an Irish prospector called Paddy Hannan who discovered gold in 1893. Within days of staking his claim, the surrounding bushland was swamped with hundreds of prospectors as gold fever spread across the mid-west of Australia. From a humble selection of wooden huts, Kalgoorlie grew quickly, and although relatively small, is now classed as a city. It lives and breathes gold and many of its inhabitants work nearby, in an area colloquially known as the Super Pit. Everyone in Kalgoorlie knows the price of gold, in the same way that mothers always know the price of a loaf of bread.

A controlled blast at the Super Pit

When some of the original tenements from the early workings became too dangerous, too deep and too uneconomical to mine they were purchased by the entrepreneur Alan Bond in the late 1980s. The decision was then made to use open cut mining, to systematically go through each and every tonne of earth in what is known as the golden mile, due to the abundance of precious metal found in the area. The manmade hole is now so large that it can be seen from space, hence its nickname of the Super Pit.

The mining company that owns the Super Pit runs its operations 24 hours per day, seven days a week, hauling thousands of tonnes of earth from the pit floor to the crushers and screens and annually produces about 800,000 ounces of gold per year. Over the decades, abandoned shafts have been discovered as the Super Pit gets deeper, unravelling discarded pieces of machinery and equipment used by the pioneer miners a century before.

With Kalgoorlie confirmed as our destination, all I had to do was locate my rucksack and walking shorts. They were still in the garage, hanging from hooks on the wall as a reminder of my gap year travel with Fran. The rucksack was coated in a fine sheen of mildew and my trusted walking shorts were encrusted with dried mud from long forgotten mountain trails. I unhooked the walking trousers and traced my fingers along the patchwork of stitches holding the worn material together. A tailor in Zanzibar had performed major surgery on the worn fabric after they had ripped on the upper slopes of Kilimanjaro and I didn't have the heart to discard them when we reached Australia.

They still fitted, just! Australia had softened me a little. Maybe it was the large amount of time spent driving to work each day or the fast food treats and socialising each weekend. I knew the answer. Middle age had crept up on me and I was no longer able to stay slim without effort. I slipped on the shorts and headed down to the beach for a run. It was late spring and mornings were no longer cool and crisp. Within weeks, the temperatures could be creeping towards the forties if the wind came from the eastern interior. I ran hard, my mind racing with thoughts of adventures long since vanished. As I sprinted along the water's edge, I thought back to the lioness charging, the midnight scramble towards the summit of Kilimanjaro and lazy days floating down the Amazon. I stopped at the marina wall, fighting for breath and bent over to suck in the warm air. I was ready for my next adventure.

Alan, Sam and Blake arrived from the UK winter, eager for sunshine and excitement. They hadn't aged in the few years since we had last met. Paler maybe, but no new wrinkles. Blake had stretched, as all boys do when you haven't seen them in a while, but his mischievous giggle still remained. Sam was still a mass of blonde curls, hugs and bright smiles. Alan hadn't changed. Still the same firm handshake, cheeky grin, shaved head and thirst for adventure. This was their first meeting with Noah. At nine months of age, he was busy exploring his new world and the arrival of Blake was perfect. It felt like he had an older brother and they bonded immediately.

Within days of touchdown, Alan and Sam experienced the delights of summertime Perth, including winery tours, sunset cruises, and lazy days by the pool. Just as Alan began to get itchy feet, it was time to head into the bush.

Perth domestic airport was a hive of activity. Now that the housing boom was over, the papers constantly discussed the mining boom and blamed the lack of carpark spaces on the surge in mineworkers heading to work by plane. Fluorescent orange was the new "in colour" in the terminal and most passengers in the crowded lounge were dressed for work rather than leisure. Gold, iron ore, diamonds and many other precious minerals were in global demand and those working in the resource sector were seemingly reaping the rewards.

The hour-long flight to Kalgoorlie once again confirmed that Perth is surrounded by ocean or desert. We flew due east, over the railway line, industrial estates and outer suburbs that skirt the heavily forested Perth hills. Small communities were visible in cleared areas, but as we flew, the forests dwindled into scrubland, surrounded by dried lakes shimmering in the early morning light.

My first impression of Kalgoorlie was a good one. The sky was a perfect blue and the taxi driver was a chirpy character. During the short journey from the airport to town he had plenty of advice on where to go for entertainment, places to eat and day trips. As we pulled into our guesthouse car park I asked him if he knew our guide, Geoff.

"Of course I do," he replied easily.

"Everyone knows everyone in Kal. Two degrees of separation here, mate. What do you want with him?"

I grinned and called out, "We're going on walkabout with him."

"I didn't know Geoff was a guide anymore. Where's he taking you?" There was a moment's silence as I looked at Alan then back to the driver and replied, "We aren't really sure, we just know we have to call him later this afternoon."

As he pulled away he called out, "Don't do anything silly, boys. Stay with Geoff and don't go wandering into the bush alone. It's gonna be hot out there during the next few days."

We stowed our luggage in the guesthouse and took a stroll in the early afternoon. Traffic was light and most cars that passed by were four-wheel drives but unlike their shiny city equivalents, these were coated in a fine layer of red dust. Pedestrians seemed to be a mix of transient office workers, off-duty miners and overseas visitors. The office staff wore crisp, white shirts, pointed leather shoes and walked sprightly along the clean pavements. The miners were dressed in fluorescent cotton shirts, steel toe-capped boots and long cotton trousers. They ambled at a slower pace, methodically pounding the well-kept streets. Most pedestrians avoided the glaring sun and hugged the buildings for shade and we followed suit, finding ourselves outside the town hall, next to a bronze statue.

Alan meets Paddy

It was a memorial for Paddy Hannan, the most famous Irishman in Kalgoorlie and on closer inspection he looked gaunt, probably from many years in the wilderness searching for gold. Despite the acclaim of finding and staking claim to one of the largest gold deposits in the world, Paddy Hannan died in 1925 with an estate of just £1,402. After a quick photo with Paddy's statue, we made our way to the nearest pub and on first impressions it looked deserted with just a handful of clientele sitting on the veranda. But as we crossed the wide road, Alan noticed a blackboard on the pavement depicting the animated figure of a scantily clad woman with the words, *Skimpy today 3-4* written boldly underneath.

Skimpies are a dying breed in many parts of Australia, but it was clear that the tradition of enticing workers to the pub by employing young attractive barmaids dressed in lingerie was alive in Kalgoorlie. We ventured inside, expecting to see a raucous group of miners ogling a barmaid from across the bar but were met by piped music and subdued clientele. Some were eating pub food, most were drinking middies of beer, a few played pool and two pensioners continually slotted money into an electronic games machine.

We parked ourselves on two stools and within seconds a semi-naked barmaid, dressed in an ivory-coloured basque, arrived to take our order. Her hair was pulled back in a tight bun and she had a small blue butterfly tattooed on the inside of her arm. "Yes boys, what are you after?" she asked sharply.

Alan pointed to the beer selections on display and asked innocently, "Do you have any local ales? You know, maybe a Kalgoorlie Indian Pale Ale?"

She looked over at me for a split second and then back to Alan, her freckled cheeks suddenly flushed, "We sell beer, mate. Cold beer and lots of it on tap! We got VB, Carlton Draught, Emu Export and more stubbies that you can throw a stick at. We don't sell Indian ale or whatever you call it."

Her eyes darted impatiently to a waiting customer on the far side of the bar and she shuffled her feet noisily while we mulled over the selection of lagers. While Alan read all the labels, I made a mental note not to get into conversation with her about the merits of real ale and how CAMRA are fighting an amazing battle in the UK to keep craft beer fresh, tasty and appealing.

She stayed for a few seconds, but while we dithered over the choices she moved away to serve another customer, who clearly knew what he was after. His bright orange clothes were covered in red dust, just like everything else in town. After a day working on the mine, his cropped hair had no sheen and his eyes were still hidden behind a dark pair of safety glasses. Once we realised that locally crafted beers were not on tap, it was an easy choice and with two middies of cold beer in our hands we made our way to the miner for a chat. He only had eyes for the barmaid and seemed reluctant to converse, so we diverted to the veranda and tucked into the carvery instead.

The second bar had chattier clientele and was advertised to have a skimpy at 4pm, so we were early for her, although I had the feeling it would be the same girl as next door. The resident barmaid looked attractive enough without the need to remove her T-shirt and recommended a golden ale "brewed here in the Midwest." The clientele were less distracted by the lack of a skimpy and conversation with the locals began to flow. At the third pub we were offered jobs by an off-duty maintenance supervisor, due to our electrical qualifications. "Come to Kalgoorlie and work for me," he slurred. "The gold price is going crazy, we're screaming for tradesmen and I hate to admit it, but you Poms are bloody good sparkies."

As we mulled over the fresh job offer, another miner appeared at the bar and as he waited to be served, Alan asked him what he did.

"Mate, I drive a truck at the gold mine and have just finished for the day." Alan was clearly excited and asked eagerly, "Wow. How big is it?" The miner smiled slowly and replied, "The truck or the mine?"

"Ah, both I suppose," Alan chuckled.

"The truck is a Caterpillar 793 and carries 225 tonnes per load. The mine is 3.6 km long and is the largest manmade hole in Australia. The job is boring at times, but it pays well. I spend all day driving from the pit floor to the top and back down again." The miner had been served a beer by now and took a long slurp, leaving a creamy froth on his top lip. It didn't seem to distract him and he tugged lightly at his bushy beard as he continued,

"Mate, to tell you the truth, I play music in the cab, have air-conditioning and somewhere in the middle of the day, stop for lunch. As long as I do my safety checks, and keep my mouth shut I'll be set for life within five years." He looked over at the barmaid and whispered, "That's if I don't blow it on beer and skimpies." After another swig of his beer he looked at Alan, "How much do you earn in Pommy Land?"

Before Alan could answer, the miner laughed and said, "Don't worry, Bro, Whatever it is, I earn double and only work half a year. Welcome to Australia, mate." He shook our hands, picked up his beer glass from the bar and headed to the veranda, reaching for his cigarettes as he went. Before venturing to another pub, I decided to call Geoff as the daylight was fading fast.

I ventured outside, drawn to the comforting site of Paddy Hannan and leaned against his sturdy back. For a few seconds I lingered in the evening sunshine, my head spinning lightly with happiness and alcohol. I reached for my phone and called Geoff's number. After the eighth ring it answered.

"Hi Geoff, It's Alistair, remember me?"

"Alistair who? Who are you?" My stomach knotted and I stood upright, walking away from Paddy and shielded my face from the sun.

"You remember, I called about going walkabout with you. I've got my friend over from England." His reply was gentler. "Yes, of course. I remember now. What's your name again?"

"Ali. I mean Alistair."

"When are you coming to Kal?"

"We're here now, on the 18th December like we agreed. I'm standing in the middle of town next to Paddy."

"I thought your friend was called Alan."

"He is. I'm standing next to the statue of Paddy Hannan." There was a brief pause while Geoff digested my news.

"You definitely still want to go? It'll be hot, you know."

"Yes, we're here and ready. And as for the weather, we had a heat wave in England in 1976, so should be prepared for whatever comes our way!" Geoff ignored my trip down memory lane and finished the call with a simple instruction: "Come and see me now. Take a taxi to the township and we'll talk."

We found a cab on the nearest street corner and as we climbed into the back seats, the driver asked, "Where to, guys?" Alan chirped, "Hello mate, can you drop us off at the Aboriginal Township please." The driver craned his head towards us, his eyes wide. "Are you serious, mate?" Alan grinned, "Yes, we're going on walkabout…" Before Alan had a chance to explain our plan, the driver interrupted, his deep voice steady and clear. "You've been watching too many Crocodile Dundee films, mate. The only walkabout going on around here is the locals crawling from one bloody pub to another. White men don't go to the townships. Especially not half-pissed Poms."

I asked, "Do you know an Aboriginal elder called Geoff?"

His voice altered a little, its gruffness easing, "Yes, mate, a decent man and his wife is a champ."

"Well, that's who we're visiting and he knows we're coming." His eyebrows scrunched while he mulled over the news and then he replied, "Ok. I'll drop you, but take my card. If you try and walk back to Kalgoorlie afterwards you're obviously dafter than you both look. Don't call me after eight as I won't come. I've got better things to do than track down Poms who wanna go walkabout in the dark."

The township was not far out of town and a concrete pillar marked its entrance, with the name embedded in the coarse rock. Just below was a faded poster that read, "Alcohol prohibited in the township. Always say no to drugs. Respect your family and they will respect you."

The taxi driver reiterated his promise to return if we called soon and dropped us off in a clearing by the gravel road. As we made our way into the centre of the township, the distinct sound of singing grew louder. It was coming from a clearing in the gum trees and I could just make out the words to *Silent Night*, getting louder with each tentative step that we took. Most residents were lounging on chairs or rugs under the canopies of trees and on closer inspection; they seemed to be either women or young children. The men stood mainly on the outskirts of the grass area, their backs resting on the bleached white trunks as they listened to the music. In the distance I could make out the silhouette of a group of children in the playground, unaware that their antics had kicked up a cloud of red dust. The setting sun ignited each tiny speck, creating an aurora around their dark gangly shapes as they ran, leapt, danced and played in the final remnants of daylight.

The township was built in a large corral, with dark brick homes on the perimeter and a red brick community building in the centre. It was hard to believe we were just a fifteen-minute drive from one of the largest gold mines on earth, but few of the riches from the golden mile seemed to have found their way into the community. The houses were simple affairs surrounded by metal fences. They looked tired and weathered, maybe from years of extreme temperature or a lack of maintenance.

Township House

In the middle of the grassed area, a makeshift stage had been erected with several rows of plastic chairs lined up in anticipation for the locals to enjoy their carols by candlelight. This was the first time since arriving in Australia that I felt acutely different. It was obvious we didn't belong. A pale-faced, head-shaven, six foot Englishman and his smaller sidekick, me. Everyone else was Aboriginal and their glistening black skin was in deep contrast to our blotched faces and sunburnt necks. The sun was casting long shadows across the parched grass now and the heat of the day refused to budge. I was in need of water and a toilet stop, but neither seemed available, so I ignored the brain signals and kept on walking.

We made our way past local residents and greeted them, but I sensed a feeling of unease, especially from the men, who stared coldly as we walked past. Most seats were devoid of spectators, except for a few women sitting together in the second and third rows. As they sat and listened to the music, toddlers crawled through the chair legs, giggling as they played hide and seek in the grass. We arrived just in time to hear the last verse of *Silent Night* and found two vacant chairs in the front row.

When the next song finished, the singer announced that a special guest had arrived and all heads turned to the roar of a motorbike at the town entrance. Father Christmas had come to town, his sack filled with sweets for the kids. During the interlude, children appeared from every angle, surrounding Father Christmas who just managed to penetrate the excited throng and revved safely away. He then completed a circuit of the town, throwing sweets as youngsters ran alongside, laughing loudly and calling for more.

During the excitement, we had left the seats to watch and while heading back, heard our names being called from the stage. A man in a loud checked shirt and baggy trousers was grinning and waving us over. He had a thick mass of frizzy hair, a bushy beard, wore square-rimmed glasses and was probably the same weight as me and Alan combined. Geoff had found us.

As we approached he called out, "Welcome, friends. I hope you're enjoying the evening. Thanks for coming. Please stay and listen for a while but don't stray too far from the seats."

Geoff's wife was one of the performers and after a brief

greeting, she returned to the stage to prepare for a duo. I sensed that she was a pivotal part of the community, as was Geoff. As Father Christmas completed his round, we made small talk and tried to confirm our plan for the morning. Geoff explained, "I will meet you in the town centre at nine o'clock, my friends. You don't need anything except a swag, a torch and a knife if you have one."

His ample girth was not what I had expected in a bush tucker guide, but it was clear from his mannerisms that he had a warm heart. A small crowd gathered nearby, waiting for him to finish talking and it was apparent that he was a man in demand. Just before we departed he reiterated, "Go and listen to the music for a while, then it will be time to leave. But please don't wander around the community."

By the fifth carol we were getting fidgety and part way through *We Wish You a Merry Christmas*, Alan tapped me on the knee. My bladder was complaining and I was constantly licking my lips. It was time to go, but as we left our seats, Geoff was nowhere to be seen. What we should have done at this point was head directly for the entrance and call our taxi driver. For some unknown reason, I convinced Alan that an evening stroll through the community to wish everybody a happy Christmas would be a spirited initiative.

The first house we reached was in total darkness, so we continued to the second, just as *We Wish You a Merry Christmas* finished. In the silence between songs we found ourselves outside a front garden. With no street lights nearby, it was hard to see far, but a porch light was enough to show that there were a few people outside the front of the house. Some were sitting quietly, others lying in sofas and a few more scattered on the lawn as though they were sleeping deeply. I called out, "Merry Christmas" just as Geoff appeared from the gum trees, panting slightly.

A deep voice called from the darkness, "Nothing to see here, white boy. Now bugger off."

Geoff called out, "Hey, I told you to go home. Come now, please." He silently escorted us to the main road, and waved us out of town a few minutes later. Our taxi driver was also quiet during the return trip to Kalgoorlie, but as we pulled over next to the statue of Paddy, he said. "Well, I bet that was an eye-opener for you both. Don't try to understand their ways, mate. Geoff is a goodun' and is trying his best. Aboriginals are a complicated subject in Australia. Just enjoy your time, respect Geoff and do the right thing."

We completed our pub crawl and at midnight Alan pushed me in an abandoned shopping trolley towards a pink and white building called Questa Casa. Looking more like a tin shed than the oldest brothel in Australia, we knocked on the door and asked if we come in for a tour and a cup of tea. The stern doorman took one look at our form of transport, shook his head from side to side, muttered something under his breath and slammed the door shut in our faces.

We woke to another clear sky and devoured the in-house orange juice while listening to the news. Perth airport was experiencing flight delays and the weathergirl promised a high of 38 degrees by mid-morning. After breakfast we made our way into the town, which was eerily quiet after the hustle and bustle of the previous evening. Most cars that passed by were four-wheel drives, covered in red dirt. I made a mental note to see if Kalgoorlie had a car wash as there was definitely a business case for one. Alan woke me from my daydream when he asked, "Ali, how much do you know about Geoff?" I looked up at his face and grinned, "As much as you do."

"Will he turn up?" I smiled again and replied enthusiastically, "Absolutely." Alan chuckled, but for a brief moment he had a rare, serious look, "I reckon we need to buy all our own water. Just in case."

We emerged from the nearest corner shop, laden down with large plastic bottles of warm mineral water and ambled to the agreed meeting place. Traffic flow was still light, with Toyota Land Cruisers still outnumbering hatchbacks. I saw no one on a bicycle, no children skateboarding, no motorbikes and just a handful of pedestrians. The sun was climbing steadily now, its powerful rays forcing us to don hats to protect our shaved heads. The next off road vehicle didn't continue, but veered left and parked up. At the wheel was Geoff, his wild hair a mass of frizz and curls and he shouted out across the empty street. "What you guys got water for? We have plenty!"

Riding shotgun was another man, far younger, probably early twenties. They both got out of the car and Geoff introduced him as Ben, his son. Aboriginals do not attempt bone-crunching handshakes. It's not their custom. Ben was softly spoken, as was his handshake. His soft curls were trimmed short and most were hidden behind a bright red baseball cap. He helped load our luggage onto the roof rack and then silently returned to the front seat. Geoff remained outside on the pavement.

"You English going somewhere afterwards?" Alan looked at me, then back to Geoff and smiled. "No, Geoff, just back to Perth."

"Why did you pack for a month and bring so much water?" He patted Alan on the back and chuckled, "Only joking my friends, hop in, it's time to go walkabout." We drove past the closed pubs, their blackboards for skimpies now safely stashed inside and within minutes we were on the outskirts of town and still hadn't passed any pedestrians. "Does nobody ever walk in Australia anymore?" I thought. As we pulled off the main road onto a narrow track surrounded by trees, Alan called out, "What's the plan for today?"

Geoff replied, "I'm taking you into the bush." Alan's retort was instant, "I know that but which bit of the bush. It looks all the same to me." Geoff chuckled and replied, "That's the problem with you white men. You're not looking properly. Look, here's our track now."

I didn't see a track, just a straggled row of wild bushes. Geoff slowed, turned off the bitumen and drove straight through them, laughing as we bounced around in the backseats. On the other side of the bushes was more scrubland but Geoff seemed to have a sixth sense of where to drive and ploughed forward. It was too noisy for meaningful conversation so for the first hour we sat in the back as the Toyota weaved through a labyrinth of trails.

Initially, I tried to gauge our direction of travel by watching the sun, but the rising heat inside the car eventually distracted me. The air inside was filling with airborne particles of dirt, sucked in through a worn filter and the cooling fan did little to appease the harsh temperature. It was then that I realised my personal water bottle was stowed in the roof rack with my rucksack. The large water bottles that Alan had purchased were rolling across the floor so I leant down to grab one. Geoff caught the movement in his rear view mirror and called out, "Good idea, Alistair. Pass the water forward, please."

I took a large gulp and passed the plastic container forward. Initially he sat it between his legs, and then took long sips between undulations in the rough track. By the time we had trampled five more bushes the bottle was drained. He passed it back and laughed out loud, "Good job you English bought water, hey!"

Ben remained quiet, listening to music through his earphones as we drove into the unknown. The sun was high by now and my stomach was demanding food. I had a stash of gingernuts in my rucksack for emergency situations, plus a banana in my day bag, which I sensed, was already squashed. Alan seemed calm, his eyes shut as the Toyota hurtled across the rutted path, unperturbed by the sheen of red dirt settling on his sweaty scalp. With impeccable timing, Geoff slowed the car and called out, "Lunch time, boys."

The vehicle came to a stop and we clambered out. We were in dense scrubland, with no obvious sign of a track and it seemed to me that Geoff was forging his own path into the wilderness. He opened the boot, pulled out a shovel and a knife, and then handed them to Alan. "Ok, now we'll dig for witchetty grubs. I hope you're both hungry."

Witchetty grubs live in the root of the witchetty tree and for thousands of years have been an important part of the Aboriginal diet during their Walkabouts. They are bursting with protein and a readymade meal to any nomads who know where to forage. A thin layer of coarse grass covered the base of the tree and we got down on our hands and knees to scrape away the groundcover. Alan was given the task of digging out the dried red mud and within minutes he had exposed the gnarled roots.

Geoff ran his fingers along one of the roots to a section

that had swelled, and explained, "This is where the grub lives." He asked Alan to gently tap the wider section with the side of the knife and as he did, the swelling reduced as the grub eased from the hollow end of the root. It plopped into Alan's hand and for a few moments we studied the strange creature. It looked like a plump hairless caterpillar, without legs. It was greyish brown, squidgy to touch and obviously irresistible to Geoff as he could no longer wait while we analysed the placid creature. He took it from Alan, popped it into his mouth, chewed slowly for a few seconds and pronounced, "Delicious. Now it's your turn."

We all took turns at digging for roots and found enough grubs to fill a small plate.

While we had been tapping them from the roots, Ben had started a small fire and after rinsing the end of the shovel with our mineral water, placed it in the heart of the flame. Once hot, he seared the grubs and offered them up for eating. They slid down easily, crunchy on the outside, soft in the middle with an aftertaste of muddy walnuts.

After such a simple lunch, I needed more sustenance and handed around my emergency ration of gingernut biscuits. I tried eating another grub, this time between two biscuits, in the hope of creating an improvised custard cream. I decided afterwards that witchetty grubs were best for emergencies and went in search of squashed banana and mineral water, in an attempt to wash away the bitter aftertaste. As I gulped the remnants of banana, Geoff put the tools back in the car and asked, "You boys still hungry? Me too. Let's go."

As we continued our journey, I was never sure if Geoff was following ancient game trails passed down from his ancestors, or just trail blazing through impregnable bush in the hope of finding a place to hunt and camp. My doubts were quelled when we came to a wide escarpment at the edge of a dried riverbed and stopped the car. He smiled and called out, "Come friends, I will show you a special place."

As we walked along the rocky outcrop he spoke bluntly to us, "You won't understand most of what I say because you are white men and not connected with the land. But I will tell you anyway. This is my ancestral land. I know every rock, tree, and game trail. My family have hunted here for generations and contrary to what you read and hear, most Aboriginals are still connected with the environment."

Until recently, most Aboriginals had an affinity with the land that most westerners have long forgotten or never had. I am no expert on the effects of colonisation on indigenous populations, but after four years in the country this was the first Australian I had met who talked as though he was truly part of the land and the environment.

He spoke briefly about the Dreamtime, but his voice rose and fell as we clambered over rocks and made our way to the dried riverbed below. The landscape had changed. A dried lake shimmered in the distance, its parched red bed waiting for the rains. A movement in the distance caught my eye. It was heading towards the tree line and by the way it moved, was four legged. "It's a dingo," Geoff explained. "Or maybe just a wild dog. No one knows the difference anymore. Come on, let's go. I'm hungry."

I stayed for a few seconds and watched the wild creature. It seemed to sense my eyes were upon it and stopped at the edge of the trees to look back. For a few seconds we stared at each other. Half-dingo, half-wild dog at the tree line and me, half-English, partly Irish, partly Scottish and now living in Australia. Maybe we were not so different after all. Both a bit mixed up and both searching for a place to call home.

As I made my way back to the vehicle I thought back to Geoff's comments about white men not having a true affinity with the land. It was a sweeping statement, but hadn't been said in malice. I knew it wasn't true and had met many people in Ecuador who were determined to restore the ravaged jungles and many of these passionate individuals were from western countries. To Geoff it was just a simple fact that most white people were out of sync with the environment and no further discussion about the Dreamtime took place during our trip.

By mid-afternoon we were trailblazing through rockier country and after numerous sightings of wallabies, Geoff slowed down in search of dinner. Just as we rounded a slight bend in a shallow valley he jerked to a stop and called out excitedly, "Hey, there's a goanna. See?" He pointed through the windscreen but all I could see was stunted trees, red earth and granite boulders scattered across the savannah.

"There it is. Just there," he whispered. The more he pointed, the less I saw and Alan shook his head in agreement. Geoff got out of the car and quietly made his way to the bonnet and once more pointed towards the boulders.

"Can you see it now?" he mouthed. I looked across at Alan and he shrugged his shoulders. Geoff was getting agitated now and Ben found the episode amusing, grinning as we strained forward to locate the lizard. Geoff returned and stuck his head through the front window. "You need to look with bush eyes, not city eyes. Watch where I am pointing." I was determined to spot it and wound the window down, forced my head and torso out and scanned the rocky outcrops. All I could see was the same as before.

Geoff returned to the side of the bonnet, picked up a large rock and held it high. He looked towards us and whispered, "I'll throw this nearby to scare it off. When it lands you watch it run." He threw the rock in a high arc towards a patch of stunted bushes, where it landed with a soft thud and clattered across the boulders. Nothing moved.

He walked over to where the rock had landed, knelt down and picked up an iguana by the tail. The lizard flopped by his side, its head dangling close to the floor as Geoff proudly held it aloft for us to see, "I'm not a good shot," he bellowed. "I've knocked it out, but I think we'll have it for dinner."

In one swift motion he held firmly onto the tail and spun the creature in a perfect arc where its head landed squarely on the bonnet. The impact killed the iguana immediately, its skull split into two. He opened the back door, tossed the iguana next to Alan's feet and chuckled, "Here's our starters for dinner."

The area must have been a perfect habitat for iguanas as we pulled over a few minutes later and watched as another lay peacefully on a granite outcrop, soaking up the mid-afternoon sunshine. He was far bigger than the first and lifted his head to investigate the droning noise from the diesel engine. Geoff had his rifle ready and took a shot from his window, with deadly accuracy. Within seconds we had a second iguana laying by our feet.

"It's time to find a place to camp," Geoff declared. "Do you have any more of that nice bottled water?"

An hour before sunset, we located a wide open area which Geoff affirmed would be our campsite. Once again, Ben had a fire going within minutes and as the shadows lengthened, Alan and I explored the area. Kangaroos kept their distance, bouncing away from view as soon as we disturbed their resting spot. The land nearby was littered with the remnants from human habitation, left behind by prospectors, campers and nomads. Each contour in the land contained something from the past. A tin mug, now home to an army ant, smashed cups, broken beer bottles, rusted tin cans and fragments of faded clothes.

Further exploration revealed numerous bore holes and the visible remains of an abandoned tenement. For a few minutes we kicked at the dirt, hoping for signs of gold, but Geoff called our names from afar and our brief exploration was over. It was time for dinner.

As the sun sunk dipped below the earth, the cloud of flies that had constantly hovered around our eyes finally abated, allowing us to talk without waving our hands. Compared to suburbia, the open sky seemed vast, with no buildings to mask the empty horizon that was now ablaze in colour. Far above, a thin band of high-level cloud turned from white to pink to velvet red as the sky flared briefly before darkness descended.

During sunset, Geoff called us over to the fireside and explained how to prepare iguanas for cooking. He broke off a small twig from a nearby bush, ensuring it had a barb and then split a small hole just below the throat of the smallest animal. "You push the twig down into its belly, twist gently a few times and then pull the guts out, which will be entwined around the barb. Easy, eh? Ok, I have beans and pasta to prepare. You boys are in charge of the meat. When they're gutted, lay them on the edge of the fire to cook slowly.

Alan prepares dinner

With surprising ease we gutted the lizards, pulling their entrails out in a single stroke with the barbed twig. Geoff returned and explained that the guts would entice ants, snakes, wild dogs or dingos and asked us to hurl them away from camp. I walked away from the fire, holding the fresh entrails with a stick and headed into the darkness. My head torch picked out two large kangaroos in the distance, their ears perked in anticipation as I came nearer. They took flight, crashing through the bush and as the world turned silent I switched off my light for a few seconds. The faint glow from the fire failed to reach me and just like my time in Africa, I once more felt like an explorer. This time I was not in the wilds of Botswana, but an hours' flight from the largest city in Western Australia.

We ate in silence around the camp fire. I was too tired for small talk and too hungry to complain about overcooked pasta. The iguana was delicious, as all food is to a ravenous person. It tasted like chicken used to before hormones were introduced and its earthy flavour complemented the warm baked beans and sticky pasta. With no moon or manmade light, the night was as black as I had hoped. At the edge of camp, Alan and I lay on our swags and gazed up at the Milky Way, eager to point out shooting stars and the Southern Cross. As we searched for satellites, Geoff appeared from the bush, his heavy footsteps intruding on the still of night. He was holding one of our bottles of water, its final contents swilling in the bottom.

"Cheers for today," Alan called.

"No worries, my friends, sleep well. I have swept the camp clear of ants and etched a mark around the perimeter. Don't worry. Nothing will cross the line."

I didn't quite know what he was expecting to come into camp, but guessed he meant unwelcome wildlife. I was unsure how a slight indent in the earth would stop an army of ants or an inquisitive snake and was too tired to dwell on the fact that the Australian outback is home to some of the deadliest wildlife on the planet. Alan seemed unperturbed, happy to read by head torch while I lay on the ground, swaddled deep inside the swag and searched for one more shooting star in the night sky.

As I drifted to sleep I thought back to my previous travel adventure, sleeping under the stars in Africa and South America. I dreamt of Carlos, my Peruvian guide and his trusty donkeys who I had nicknamed Angus and

Oliver. Where were they all now? In my reverie Carlos appeared from the wilderness, his two donkeys safely tethered after a day's trekking across the Andes. He whispered something to me in Spanish, but I didn't understand, so he took my hand and led me to a wide river, surrounded by snow-capped peaks. As I sat by the water's edge, he expertly cast into clear pools, plucking trout from the swirling eddies. He walked towards me smiling, the fresh trout glistening in his hands, but as he came closer, the dream began to fade and I could no longer hear his words.

Another noise was nearer, a shrill buzzing sound that sucked me from dreamland and cut the connection. I could feel the first light ebbing through my closed eyelids and reached out to automatically turn off the alarm clock. The dream was over and it was time for work. I opened my eyes and all became clear. The sun was low on the horizon, Geoff was standing close by looking down at me, and the first fly of the day was in my ear.

On the afternoon of day two we drove on bitumen for the first time since leaving Kalgoorlie. The morning had been a lazy affair, with a walk in the surrounding bushland to explore abandoned tenements, but as the sun rose, the clapped out air-conditioning in the car suddenly became very appealing.

"Where to today then, Geoff?" Alan asked once more.

"Into the bush, my friends," was the reply as we left camp and headed straight for the nearest shrubs. All morning we bounced across rutted tracks in search of our next dinner. Geoff kept mumbling something about kangaroos, but the shimmering horizon gave no clues to their whereabouts. Each hour he would call for a fresh water bottle, as the temperature and dust inside the cabin rose. I dozed off, woken by a gentle tap on the shoulder from Alan. "Hey, Ali, wake up. Look. It's a road."

I opened my eyes and saw a fence, a gate and a scrawny goat. I wiped sweat from my brow then looked again and they were gone. Up ahead was a single bitumen road, its black tarmac pitted and gnarled from sunshine and neglect. "Where are we, Geoff?" I heard myself say.

"In an old mining town called Kookynie. I bet you boys want a beer, eh?"

Alan looked over at me, cracked a mischievous smile and said, "Sounds like a plan, Geoff. I thought you'd never ask!" I wasn't sure if Geoff was joking, as the chances of finding a pub seemed remote, but the appearance of a roundabout bought hope. The first signpost in two days revealed our distance to the nearest small towns, most of which were small settlements in the vast interior.

Alistair and Alan on their way to the Kookynie Hotel

As Geoff slowed, I opened my guide book. A quick scan revealed that the population of Kookynie was just 13, but there was no sight of anyone as we entered the main street. Maybe the residents were all in the pub or out in the wilderness searching for gold? We passed a row of abandoned brick houses, their sealed windows hiding all secrets of the original inhabitants. My book referred to Kookynie as a mining town, but as we drove down the desolate strip, there was little sign of activity.

Up ahead, there was one building that stood out from the dust and abandonment. The Kookynie Hotel was like an oasis in the desert, complete with hanging baskets in full bloom. Geoff parked the car and we all got out to stretch our legs. The road was devoid of traffic and nothing stirred in the heat, except the persistent flies. "You boys go inside. Take your time," Geoff called out as they wandered into the bush for a toilet break. It was best not to question them. Aboriginals and pubs are not always a good mix and if they didn't want to come in, even for lemonade, then we wouldn't try to persuade them.

The saloon door was prised open by a boot-sized lump of iron ore and the distinct sound of Glen Campbell ebbed through the fly mesh from the darkened passageway. Alan pushed open the mesh door and we walked inside. Instead of looking like an establishment on its final legs it was neatly furnished and ready for business. A diverse selection of beers, spirits, cigarettes, potato chips and peanuts were displayed across the back of the bar. For those in need of other items, there was a limited choice of tinned food, magazines, newspapers and on one shelf sat a single packet of two-minute noodles. The walls were decorated with retro images of Australian football posters, beer mats and faded postcards from across the world. On one wall a mounted stag's head looked like it had been dragged across the hedgerows of Devon, before being shipped to the outback.

We each sat on a bar stool, just as a barman appeared

from the back room and greeted us with a friendly, "G'day." He was about fifty, quietly spoken with a stringy grey beard and asked us what we were after. Alan gazed at the beers on tap, looking for something that was obviously not there but I admired his tenacity.

"Hello, mate, do you have any locally brewed beer?" The barman put his hand on the nearest beer tap, which was coated in ice, and looked Alan in the eye.

"We got plenty of beer here, mate. All ice cold. If you like exotic stuff I can sell you an expensive bottle of lager that Mexicans supposedly drink. Other than that, you can take your pick."

The choice was limited, but in a ghost town you can't be picky. My guess was that after 12 hours sifting through dirt to find a speck of gold you don't care so much about taste. It just has to be cold enough to shred a layer of skin on the way down. We each chose a pint of Swan Draught and as he poured, I enquired about the two-minute noodles as our evening meal was by no means guaranteed.

While Alan chatted with the barman about the merits of warm English beer, I took a walk to the toilet, passing framed photos of days long past when Kookynie was a pioneer town in the grip of a gold frenzy. It would have been an amazing time to be in mid-west Australia, akin to the gold rushes in the USA. The pictures were in excellent condition, as was the decor and it was clear that the owner was very proud of the hotel's heritage.

By the time I returned, another drink had been served and the barman was enjoying the banter. As I mentioned before, Alan is an asset to any adventure trip as he can cajole most people into an easy conversation. As they talked about the latest price of gold and the last great discovery, I studied the packet of noodles. They were five months out of date, but by nightfall, if it was either these or witchetty grub custard creams, I knew which one would win.

I put down the noodles and tuned into the lively chat from the barman. "Yes, there were thirteen people in town. But that's down to ten now and would you believe, they don't all get on. Five live to the left of the pub about a kilometre away, three to the right and two more come and go with the wind." Alan grinned and took a long sip of his beer as the barman continued, "No one can remember why they fell out. Probably about mining rights or a card game or something stupid like that. So the ones who live on the left come in on a Monday night, and the others sit right where you guys are. They don't bother so much at the weekends as it's filled with blow-ins, like you two. Most Saturdays the place is filled with retired Australians and overseas visitors on escorted day coach trips from Kalgoorlie."

It was clear that these visitors were his financial lifeline, but the nomadic Australians were the ones I wanted to meet. They were an elusive bunch and as we contemplated a third beer I thought about my next adventure, in search of these larrikins.

Before leaving, the barman gave us a quick history lesson and revealed that he was also the hotel owner. With a sense of pride he rolled off a series of facts and figures about the glory days of gold mining in the area. During the boom years at the turn of the twentieth century, the town had 3,500 residents, eleven hotels and an active train line to Kalgoorlie. It also had a racecourse, delicatessens, factories, a red-light district and the first swimming baths in Western Australia.

The only reason that such a large populous would reside in the harsh interior was due to the abundance of precious minerals, but constant flooding, fluctuating spot prices and richer pickings elsewhere, resulted in a mass exodus. Lone prospectors still roam the area, spending weeks, months and years in the wilderness, searching for gold and other precious stones.

As the owner spoke, I wondered if Paddy Hannan had ever drank at the same bar where we were now sitting. I could imagine the animated conversations each evening, as migrants, vagabonds, prospectors and entrepreneurs discussed the latest gold findings, each tale taller than the last.

We thanked the owner and stood to leave. He was about to prepare dinner for a coach load of Japanese tourists en route from Kalgoorlie and it felt good knowing the hotel would soon be alive with the sound of chatter. We waved farewell and stepped out of the dark interior into bright sunshine. Before coming to Kalgoorlie, it had been many years since I had walked out of a pub with Alan during the middle of the day. A lad's holiday in Tenerife would have been our previous attempt at a lunchtime session and that had been a decade earlier. We were still clinging to hair at the time and had taken a holiday from the car factory to gallivant around the island. But the factory was shut, our hair was long gone and here we were now on the other side of the world in search of new adventures.

We set up camp that afternoon by a dam and spent the evening fishing for freshwater crustaceans called yabbies, using a net and trap that Geoff had stashed on the roof rack in preparation. Using remnants of iguana as bait, Geoff entrusted Alan and me with pulling the lines in at regular intervals. The water must have been teeming with the creatures, who were still nibbling at the stringy meat as we emptied each catch into a waiting bucket. On closer inspection they looked to be the direct link between prawn and crab and that evening, as we feasted on boiled yabbies, the two-minute noodles became a distant memory.

No amount of toothpaste could remove the strong taste of fish from my mouth, but out in the wilds no one cared. Once again we crawled into our swags for a deep sleep under the stars, and this time my dreams were serene.

On the morning of the third day, Geoff seemed pensive as we prepared to leave camp.

"Is everything ok?" I asked tentatively.

My words seemed to shake him out of a daydream and he turned to look at me, his frizzy hair now totally wild and unkempt. He smiled, pointed to the bushland and in an animated voice, called out, "Today we're gonna get a roo."

Geoff prepared his rifle and after a breakfast of grilled yabbies we headed into the bush in high anticipation. All morning we drove along ancient game trails, but the kangaroos were elusive, either resting undetected under trees, or too far on the horizon to reach. The relentless bouncing across the rutted landscape affected the mood of the passengers, as Geoff's obsession became a quest for us all. Basking iguanas were ignored in favour of distant kangaroos, but each burst across the bush ended in dismay.

We nibbled gingernuts for morning tea and by mid-afternoon I was looking for witchetty trees and while doing so, spotted a lethargic bird foraging in the scrub.

Geoff recognised it as a wild bush turkey and as might be expected, it stood little chance against a high velocity rifle. At lunchtime, it supplemented the two-minute noodles and baked beans that we had during an impromptu stop. As soon as the food was devoured, Geoff was eager to move on, convinced that the bush turkey had changed our luck. I washed down a seared turkey thigh with a swig of mineral water and returned to the back seat with Alan.

The sun was at its zenith now and the shrilled sound from the air-conditioner fan seemed to lower the temperature inside the car. It was the first time since leaving Kalgoorlie that I realised we all smelt. Alan was wearing the same T-shirt as the day before and his unshaven face was smeared in red dust and turkey grease. He grinned, probably seeing that I was in similar shape and returned to his travel book as we rolled with the bumps. Ben remained quiet, taking the job of riding shotgun seriously as we scanned the hazy horizon for signs of life. Geoff called for another water bottle and as Alan passed one forward, the car came to an abrupt halt. Geoff pointed into the distance and whispered, "There on the right, what can you see under the tree?"

I didn't know if he was speculating or informing us, and I daren't admit that all I could see was acres of red dirt, scrawny bushes and a tree with a torn limb. But there was something about the shape of the huge branch lying at the foot of the tree. I ignored the sweat running down my back and waved away a fly to concentrate further. There was a slight movement. A flicker. Of an ear? All small talk vanished; the only sound now, the thudding drumbeat of the diesel engine.

I thought back to Geoff's words from a few days earlier.

About looking with city eyes. I blinked the sweat away and looked once more at the gnarled branch. It was no longer a large piece of rotting timber. At last I could see an outline of what could be a head. It moved again, revealing two ears and a prominent nose as it stood to investigate the unnatural commotion. Geoff had found his kangaroo.

From my previous encounters with African wildlife, I knew that wild animals analysed every potential threat and either fought back or took flight. The alert manner in which the kangaroo stood told me that he was poised to flee but a sideways glance towards us was the last movement it ever made. Geoff had already steadied the rifle and as the animal stared, the loud crack of the rifle reverberated inside the car. Far in the distance at that moment, the kangaroo's head whipped back as it keeled over.

With ringing still in my ears, we quickly drove to the kill site as Geoff didn't want it to suffer, but there was no need for haste as his head shot had been clean. It was a fully grown grey kangaroo, now flat on its back with only half a head left. He stowed the rifle, sliced off the tail and threw it onto the rear seats, then declared with authority, "We need to find a big tree."

I was unsure why, but sensed it was the wrong time to ask questions. With simplified precision, Geoff and Ben trussed a rope around the animal then asked for help in getting it onto the bonnet of the vehicle. Alan pulled a leg and I pushed from the rear as it slid across the car and was tethered to the roof rack. Flies were already buzzing around the carcass, despite it being dead less than a minute, but they seemed to disappear as soon as we started to drive again. Within three minutes of the rifle shot we were trailblazing through bushland, searching for a big tree.

With every bump the dead kangaroo rolled back and forth, its head and torso splattering on the bonnet as Geoff scanned the pitted landscape for his required tree. It didn't take long and as the car stopped suddenly, the kangaroo's head splattered against the windscreen and the flies instantly returned. We pulled the carcass from the bonnet and with ease Geoff and Ben set up a rope and hung the animal from the thickest branch. Now I understood!

While Ben started a small fire, Geoff gutted the kangaroo, ignoring the cloud of gorging flies that hovered thick around his bushy hair. He was in the zone now, his honed knife slicing through the coarse skin to find the succulent meat. We left him with the flies and decided to set up the table and chairs in anticipation.

While cleaning the table with Alan's mineral water, Geoff appeared by my side, grinning. A lump of shimmering meat was skewered to his blade, which he flicked onto the wet surface. Another soon followed it, this time for Alan.

"Ok, boys, grab your meat and roast it in the fire."

Both chunks were still moving. They were the size of doughnuts, shiny pink and left a trail of thin blood on the table top as they quivered under the midday sun. We gorged on roasted kangaroo for the next hour and camped nearby, well away from the carcass. It was our final night and as kangaroo cubes, potatoes, carrots and local herbs simmered in the fireside pot, Geoff once again told tales of life on the land as an Aboriginal. I asked him about the Dreamtime, but he was still reluctant to elaborate. Eventually he just said, "You boys are good. I reckon if you stayed with me for a few months you would understand. But city people are always in a hurry and rarely learn." Maybe he was right. I was eager for a shower and the thought of a grilled rump steak was beginning to gnaw at the back of my mind.

Just before we turned in for the night, Geoff collected his kangaroo tail and buried it in the dying embers at the edge of the fire. He noticed me watching and smiled, "My breakfast, Ali. Out here in the bush you have to think ahead." As I lay watching for shooting stars I looked over at Alan. He was munching on a cold bush turkey fillet, chuckling softly while reading his book by torch light.

Sunrise dictates life in the bush so bright sunshine and buzzing flies meant another early start to the day. We broke camp, dampened the fire, cleaned our area and for the final time got into the car. Two kilometres down the track Geoff called out, "Alan, did you take my kangaroo tail out of the embers?"

Alan looked at him quizzically, "No, Geoff, was I meant to?"

A sharp U-turn meant that the answer was yes. After collecting the roasted tail, Geoff seemed lively and with each kilometre I could sense we were once again returning to civilisation. Fences appeared, housed with skinny goats and gaunt cattle, but the area still seemed devoid of people. Our first sighting of power lines meant that the trip was all but over. They were running parallel with a bitumen road and I knew it wasn't long until we made it back to Kalgoorlie.

After a few kilometres on the tarmac, Geoff made a small detour, driving onto another gravel road and stopping the car one last time. Ben searched in the back for remnants of tinned food, but Geoff was happy to chew on the kangaroo tail and finished off the last bottle of mineral water. He offered us a bite, but I declined, saving my appetite for a pub meal at the Exchange Hotel. By midday, the adventure was over.

Geoff drove us to his home to meet his family and then to the Aboriginal community hall, where he proudly showed us the projects he was working on. A visitors' book caught our eye and we asked if we could borrow it while we headed into town.

Our timing was impeccable. Happy Hour had just commenced and as we walked into the bar, we recognised the skimpy from our previous visit. I wasn't sure if she remembered us. Three days without a shower had left its mark, but we wore our red sheen with pride and plonked down on the nearest bar stools. The place was quiet except for a few pensioners feeding coins into a slot machine and an off-duty miner sitting alone in the corner. The barmaid came over to where we sat and asked, "Yes, boys, what are you after?" Alan scanned the beer taps and replied, "Two middies of your coldest beer, please." She looked at us again then smiled warmly. "You boys are learning fast and it looks like you've been busy since we last met."

Alan grinned and muttered something about prospecting for gold. She had heard it all before and didn't raise an eyebrow as she expertly poured two icy beers, her eyes drawn to the doorway in search of more clientele. While the chef prepared steak, mushrooms and chips we took our beers onto the veranda and wrote a poem in Geoff's visitors' book.

Out in Kalgoorlie there was a couple of blokes, one called Ben the other Geoff Stokes,
Who took some lads from the Hannan street pubs,
To sample kangaroo meat and witchetty grubs,
He promised us bush tucker and was true to his word,
So in the pot that night sat a bush turkey bird,
Yes Geoff is a legend and he showed us his home,
Showing us the places where his family once roamed,
So thanks for the experience and the education at that,
We're off home to explore the garden and hunt for the neighbour's cat.

Many thanks
Big Al and Al

9

SUNSHINE AND SHADOW

"I could not have made it this far had there not been angels along the way."
Della Reese
2006. Bunbury, Western Australia.

Sunshine and Shadow
I am pregnant
Fran whispers
With our second child
Your belly swells
As the seasons change
And leaves begin to fall
Alice is travelling soon
From England

Once more, to help
The spare room is ready
Fragrant smells and fresh linen
After a walk on the beach
Our telephone rings
There is sad news
That breaks my heart
A fire, my brother tells me
His voice distant
And Alice is gone
My mind is numb
But Fran needs me
To be strong
When the waters break
We try a home birth
For hours, in the bath
But the baby is big
And Fran is weak
In desperation
We travel at speed
To hospital, where Sebastian is born
10 pounds in weight
He is loved
And feisty
Just like Auntie Alice
His angel

10

HALF A WORLD AWAY

"By the time a man realises that maybe his father was right, he usually has a son who thinks he's wrong."
Charles Wadsworth

2007. Perth, Western Australia.

Dad couldn't legally move to Australia as too many of his siblings remained in the UK, but that didn't stop us persuading him to make the overseas trip, so that he could escape the long English winters that drove him to despair. It was the rain that wore him down. From late October until early March he hibernated, waiting for the sun to return once more. Bright winter mornings were still capable of enticing him onto the frozen golf fairways, but the bleak days used to turn him into a curtain-twitcher, cocooned inside his house. During mid-winter in the UK, I called his home number, in the hope of getting him on a flight to Australia.

"How are you, Dad?"

"I'm not well. My bones ache and I've been to the doctor again, but he just gives me more pills. I'm fed up with the rain, there's nothing to do, its dark outside and my knees are playing up."

"Well, we'd love you to visit us in Australia for a few months. You haven't seen your second grandchild, Sebastian, yet and he looks just like you." There was a slight pause, followed by a low murmur as Dad replied, "I know I should come over, but apart from seeing the kids what would I do each day?"

"Dad, where do I start? You can sunbathe by the Indian Ocean, jump in the pool, play golf alongside kangaroos, enjoy a few cold beers and most importantly, make sandcastles with your grandchildren." There was a brief silence on the line as he contemplated the proposal but I could not contain my enthusiasm and asked,

"Dad, what do you reckon? Shall I book a flight?"

"Oh, ok. I'll come over for a few weeks."

And so it happened that for three winters running my Dad spent most of November to January in his doctor's surgery and every February to April playing in the sunshine with his grandchildren in Australia.

At the arrivals section at Perth airport he would walk tentatively through the immigration doorway, carrying a small backpack whilst nervously scanning the crowds for a familiar face. He rarely felt relaxed on the flights and after landing we would hug in the airport terminal, as he muttered, "Never again."

But within a week of arriving, the sparkle would return. He would locate the beer fridge, lap up the sunshine, and tee off as kangaroos munched nearby, on the manicured fairways. In the evenings I would try to extract stories from him about his life. It was a valuable time. He shared snippets about his time in the merchant navy, and reminisced about growing up in Glasgow. I learnt more about Dad during these daily chats on the veranda than I had when living in the same town as him. By being apart, we had somehow bonded.

One February evening, my brother Matthew phoned to ask after Dad. It was the third year in a row that he had been out to visit, but getting him on a plane was proving more difficult. On this occasion he had insisted on being wheeled to the plane and had been to the doctor every week leading up to the flight, complaining of many ailments from back pain to suspected cancer of the thyroid.

I put Matthew's mind to rest. "I can see him now. He's in the garden and both boys are playing football with him." As I watched, he knelt in front of their tiny goal posts, then rolled across the grass to save the ball as his grandchildren giggled in delight. Throughout his time in Australia, there were no trips to the doctor, no discussions about his arthritis, thyroid pains or dodgy knees. All he wanted was to have his family care for him and we embraced the special times.

The point of this story is that their grandad spoilt my children rotten for three months every year. I know it's not the same as living nearby in England, but having him around for 90 days of summer was a magical time. If you move Down Under, you may be away from your parents or close family, but when they do come over it could be for many weeks or months. This is an ideal time to form strong bonds in a way that is different to back home. I'm not saying that it's better, but there is the potential to nurture precious relationships during these extended visits.

I know that when I lived in England, visits to Dad were sporadic. I would see him each week, maybe for an hour on a Thursday evening and he would come round for dinner most Sundays. During winter, life was busy for me and boring for him. So when we met, it was far from ideal. He wanted to talk about his ailments. I tried to listen and would include him in social events. It was rarely enough to satisfy us both.

When he came to visit us in Australia, many of his ailments disappeared and I saw him every day. We had evening meals together, went fishing at weekends and he enjoyed the gatherings we had with neighbours. Our new-found friends adored his quirky personality and we bonded more in those three months than a decade of weekly family gatherings in the UK.

My most precious memory is the day that he took one of the children on their first ever bus ride. Here was a three-year old and his grandad out on an adventure. As they left the house, to walk down the road towards the bus stop, I managed to hold back the tears and captured a few seconds on my video camera.

11

IN A STEW

"You cannot soar with eagles if you are walking around with chickens."
Unknown

2008. Western Australia.
Life was good until the Global Financial Crisis. Aus-

tralia was not immune to the economic tidal wave from the USA and Europe and many workers were vulnerable. At that time, I was on a fixed-term contract with a mining company. The global organisation extracted titanium from mineral sands and as luck would have it, my three years ended just as the Global Tsunami hit. The classifieds were devoid of anything meaningful and large corporations were in crisis management. I should have been wary when the only relevant online position available had been readvertised multiple times, but desperate times meant desperate measures and I called the number in the advert.

Two days later I met the HR Manager, a fresh-faced man called Nigel, with thick curly hair and a cheeky grin. Over coffee we talked about the role and my previous leadership and management experience. I proudly explained my career transition from tradesman to a Business Improvement facilitator. But my MBA studies and Six Sigma Black Belt qualification meant nothing to him. He eyed me seriously and asked, "Impressive qualifications, but can you deal with variety?"

"Of course," I replied, eager to please.

"Then you are in the right place, Alistair. Every day here is different. It's very busy and we seem to have high turnover for some reason."

As we made our way to the factory for a brief tour I shared my thoughts, hoping to impress him one final time. "In the past, I've helped make cars, caravans, titanium, furniture and bricks. Processing chickens can't be that difficult, can it"? Nigel was unusually quiet, kept walking and didn't answer. Maybe he knew something I didn't about processing chickens.

It was still dark as I drove into the carpark for my first

day's work at the chicken factory. It had been a forty-minute drive from my house and the road had been free of traffic jams and traffic lights. Moving south from metropolitan Perth had its merits. All I needed was a steady job to go with the "Down South" lifestyle and maybe a career in chickens was just the answer.

My heart was beating faster than normal as I parked the car and switched off the radio midway through a Spandau Ballet classic. I had chosen mid-eighties pop for the morning drive to keep me alert during the journey. As the music cut off instantly, the only sound was my sharp breathing as I gathered my bag and walked towards the factory entrance. My heart was still racing as I reached the main door. Everyone gets nervous on day one of a new job, but deep down I had a sense that this was not the smartest career move. But there was nowhere else to go and during the site tour with Nigel I had managed to ignore the smell of death that permeated through the chilled corridors, and had apparently asked enough smart questions to merit a job.

I could see Nigel now, strolling across the carpark towards me, his face already smiling despite the early hour. He was dressed to kill. A hair net covered his soft curls and a standard white pair of overalls hung low to his knees. It wasn't often in life I towered over other adults and I sensed that Nigel had never yet needed to shave.

"G'day Alistair. So the interview didn't scare you off?"

I felt unsure if this was meant to be a joke, but forced a chuckle, just in case. The carpark was filling up fast now and workers quietly walked past, with some nodding to Nigel as they made their way to the factory door. The majority looked to be migrants from Asia and were probably linked to some type of work visa. I tried to suppress the thought that the company exploited cheap labour and smiled as they passed by. A squeal of tyres revealed a latecomer, as a cheap transit van jerked to a halt and half a dozen Asians dashed towards the entrance, waving to Nigel as they ran through the puddles.

Nigel smiled back and then called out to a man marching across the carpark, who by the look of the giant strides he was taking, seemed eager to be somewhere else.

"Hey, Malcolm, wait up, this is Alistair!"

During the interview I had heard that a man called Malcolm was going to be my boss but until that moment we had never met. He walked over and we shook hands. It was firm but quick as his eyes were elsewhere, checking out the workers as they went through the doorway. It was first light and already he seemed on edge.

"Hi, Alistair. I haven't got time to talk as there's a problem with a freezer."

He turned away from me and looked at Nigel, "Get Alistair some overalls and a hair net and then meet me later."

His spoke rapidly and didn't wait for a reply as he pushed open the main factory door and headed inside. We followed suit and once again the conflicting smells of death and disinfectant wafted through the main corridor. The temperature had dropped immediately and no amount of night shift cleaning could mask the stench of carnage that clung to the clammy walls. The factory was coming to life now, all workers dressed in white overalls as they headed to their workstations.

The main corridor linked all the processing rooms and was soon filled with employees. Some workers were pushing metal trolleys filled with cartons of frozen chickens; others were travelling in the opposite direction pushing crates of dissected chickens. It didn't take long for their faded white overalls and plastic gum boots to become tainted with fresh blood, but no one seemed bothered. I smiled at a few as they passed, but received blank looks in reply. The concrete floor was uneven, and broken trolley wheels snagged in the dips, causing operators to call out in frustration, but no one seemed to hear their cries.

I shivered constantly and made a mental note to buy some thermal underwear as business shirts and smart trousers were obviously not a requirement for my job anymore. The workers continued to pass by, but most seemed unaware of my presence and were eager to keep moving. Maybe it was the biting cold? Or was it the surveillance cameras that protruded from every intersection in the corridor?

I had noticed them during my site tour but hadn't realised how many there actually were. The factory looked like a Big Brother game show without the camaraderie. I gazed at the cameras and wondered what they were really designed for. Maybe workers were smuggling chicken breasts out in the dark of night. They must have been installed for security reasons, but why so many?

I scanned the faces of the people as they marched past. Very few looked like locals. As two slight women walked past, chattering quietly to one another in a foreign language, I remembered a conversation with Nigel during my interview.

"We use Koreans as they're good workers, happy to work in the chicken processing industry and appreciate the above-award wages."

Above-award wages sounds appealing, but these rates are generally the minimum amount allowed by law.

Above the award could mean a few cents or a maybe a dollar or two more per hour. I didn't see any new cars in the carpark. In fact, many of the Koreans travelled together in minivans.

As I watched them push over-filled trolleys along the corridor I had a flashback to a film called Midnight Express, about life in a Turkish prison. In several scenes, insane prisoners congregated each day at a giant grinding wheel and with no reason or purpose they would grab one of the huge wooden spokes and walk silently in circles for hours. These workers had the same strained looks, pushing trolleys along the blood-stained floor, ignoring their colleagues going the opposite way and oblivious to those struggling with broken wheels and twisted frames.

My daydream ended when Malcolm marched along the corridor towards me and called out, "Alistair, let's go. I'll show you where to put your bag."

We entered a small room that smelt of raw chicken and was filled with clutter. Stacks of cardboard boxes depicting healthy plump chickens were sprawled across the floor and broken parts of machinery were dumped onto a wooden table. There was sheaths of paperwork stacked in every available spare space. Some were in folders, others dumped in piles across two other tables. I searched for room on the floor and placed my rucksack down, then turned to face Malcolm.

'Ok. Great stuff. What now?"

His phone rang, but he read the caller's name, broke the connection and looked up at me.

"This is the production office. Here's your desk and I'm over there."

My desk was full of broken machine parts and there

was no chair in sight. I looked at him quizzically. Was he some type of comedian along with Nigel? Was this the inaugural initiation test? Maybe chicken-processing managers had zany senses of humour. With all the blood, carnage and stench I could imagine why. I smiled, just in case he wasn't being serious, but he held my stare.

"Have you got a problem with your desk?"

I felt my heart race and answered, "Truthfully yes. The office is full of junk, my table is covered in crap and there's no computer or chair." For a few seconds the room went silent. His cheeks were flushed, maybe from exertion but I couldn't be sure.

"Why do you kind of people think the business world needs computers? I don't need one and neither will you."

I wasn't sure what he meant by my kind of people and opened my mouth to ask for more detail, but his phone rang again and he fled into the corridor. I looked around the room and studied my desk. The first box was full of worn bearings and metal brackets. The others were filled with discarded tools, maintenance manuals and safety induction booklets. As I began scrolling through the pages, Nigel entered and said, "Oh you found the safety induction then. Have a read and I'll test you in an hour."

I located a plastic chair under a crate of broken sprockets and settled down to read the manual and by the time I had finished my stomach was rumbling. There was no room on my desk to eat, so I pulled out the drawer. It was filled with a roll of *Fresh is Best* stickers, now yellowing with age. I threw them onto the floor as I didn't have a bin and used the drawer to place my water bottle and ham sandwich, which Fran had prepared that morning. I took a bite, lay back in the chair and waved to the overhead camera just as Nigel walked through the door.

"What are you doing? Don't wave to the cameras. He could be watching," he whispered.

"Who?" I asked innocently.

He came closer and whispered, "The owner. He watches everything from his computer console and is very keen to meet you later." Just then, Malcolm burst into the room and started looking through some paperwork near his desk. As he trawled through the folders he called out, "Alistair, I'll catch up with you soon. I've got something urgent to sort out."

I never saw Malcolm again until the next day when he raced into the office and called out that there was another emergency. A delivery of frozen chickens from Adelaide had arrived overnight by freight, but no one had checked whether the freezers had capacity. Two of them were broken and the others were loaded incorrectly. I was given the task of pulling defrosting chickens from a clapped-out freezer, and restacking them tightly together in another. Malcolm told me it should take about an hour. It took six. By home time, he explained that the guy that stacked the overnight freight had resigned at lunchtime. As I was a supervisor, it was now my problem and could not leave until it had been rectified.

With weary arms, aching shoulders, frozen limbs and dulled senses I persevered with the frozen boxes. Each attempt to drag the dense cardboard containers from the shelf onto my shoulder then onto the trolley slowly drained my strength. It was only mental stupidity and a mortgage that kept me from hurling the chicken thighs against the grey walls and running away. Instead, I monotonously trudged from the cool room to the trailer, pushing the mangled trolley along the broken concrete as the hours passed slowly.

No amount of hot air blasting from the car heater could stem the tremor from my hands as I drove home in the dark. I was physically drained, mentally saturated and still wondered why I had not just walked out of the factory and never returned. Fourteen hours without a thanks and all because the factory was in chaos with no planning, no structure, and no idea what was happening. It was pure stubbornness that had kept me there. Plus, there was a glimmer of hope that I could instil some sense into Malcolm. Fran had a bath ready and I ate my dinner while soaking in the warm water. In seven hours I would be back in the factory and could already feel the anxiety rising in my aching stomach.

On Wednesday, the boning section was in uproar when one of the workers attacked another, leading to a boisterous end to another bloody day. On Thursday the automatic head-chopping section snapped, causing a backlog of hanging chickens waiting in anticipation. The maintenance man was asleep in his car and after I woke him he trundled over to have a poke around. Thursday was reasonable. Only one worker was sacked and with Malcolm running from crisis to crisis, I found some scrap paper and wrote out a production report to highlight where we could improve.

On Friday afternoon I was invited to meet the owner. From the moment I set eyes on his work area, it was clear that he ruled his roost in a manner akin to Victorian London. His reddened cheeks hinted of too many after dinner ports and his thick head of auburn hair sheened under the harsh florescent lights. As I approached, he puffed out his wide chest and pointed me to a nearby seat, ignoring my outstretched hand.

He was sat in front of a large screen where live images

were being shown of all the workers. I could see the maintenance man trying to unjam the head chopping machine again and on another screen was an image of workers pushing broken trolleys along the pitted corridor. It was clear by now that I was in a mad house, but the Global Financial Crisis ruled and there was nowhere to run to.

"Well, Alistair, how was your first week?" he asked.

"Actually, I think you have a few challenges but I've prepared a production, maintenance and safety report for you and Malcolm to read." His mottled cheeks darkened as he snatched the paper and set it aside on his desk.

"That's just a photocopy," I said. "It's mainly for Malcolm. But I want you to be aware that I'm used to analysing reasons why production targets aren't met. On that note, do we ever fulfil all the daily orders?"

He ignored my question as his eyes were locked onto the giant screen where a grainy image depicted two men laughing while they loaded a truck with boxes. He grabbed his phone, speed dialled and in a firm voice gave out clear instructions, "Malcolm, head over to dispatch immediately and tell the two men standing outside that if they want to joke they can clock off and look for an employer that appreciates comedians." He put down the phone and smiled brightly. "Well, that sorts out that problem. I hate lazy workers, don't you?"

I excused myself, eager to escape any further conversation. I would get more sense and a lot more enjoyment from my children. It was Friday evening and Malcolm was still running around the factory but I made a dash for freedom and halfway across the carpark heard my name being called. It was Nigel. He ran over, grinning with enthusiasm.

"Alistair, guess what. We need you to run the bagging room on Monday. The team leader just quit so you're in charge. Don't worry, I'll help you. See you Monday before six." Before I had time to answer he was trotting towards the main office.

As planned, Nigel met me at the deserted carpark on Monday morning. He was oddly quiet, with little eye contact and I sensed he was worried. But what could go wrong? We kitted out in white overalls, gum boots and obligatory hairnets and washed our hands before entering the room, which I had seen during my induction but it looked so different now. The meat separation machine had been pulled apart over the weekend to be thoroughly cleaned and was now in bits on the floor. It looked like a giant Ikea flat pack, without the instructions or tools to assemble it. I looked at the clock on the wall. It was 5.30am. We had thirty minutes to rebuild the machine before the workers and first batch of frozen chicken parts arrived.

I had never known HR managers to get so involved in production requirements, but I realised by now that Nigel was slowly losing the plot after two years at the factory. He could no longer see the cracks anymore and was seeing chaos as normality. I estimated that within a few months he would be pushing trolleys in the corridor. If I stayed more than a month I would be pushing alongside him and we could grin at each other as we passed by in the freezing corridor. Maybe those in the corridor were once supervisors and managers. I made a mental note to check their names and was broken from my daydream as Nigel called out, "Fifteen minutes to go." By now the workers were trickling into the room. Nigel had employed them all and they seemed pleased to see him and smiled enthusiastically. Two had arrived in the country over the weekend and few of the workers spoke fluent English.

The machine was ready with minutes to spare, although I realised now that it was in need of maintenance with worn parts, fraying cables and ill-fitting segments. Two Australian workers had been preparing frozen pieces of chicken and at six o'clock wheeled in an enormous steel bin containing them all.

"Here you go, Alistair. Good luck," one of them called out and his team mate pitched in, "The machine's a piece of crap and no ever makes the production target. Here's to another crazy day."

Their comments made me chuckle. It had been a long time since I had smiled and it felt good to know that I wasn't the only one that thought the place was nuts. They lifted the bin onto a small conveyor and tipped the entire contents of frozen chicken portions onto a sorting rack. It was immediately clear that the metal was twisted and had a gaping hole in one corner from a broken weld. Brine and blood swept onto the floor so I called out for a bucket to contain the innards.

I looked around proudly at this team of young Koreans, whom I had only known a few minutes. One was under the machine mopping up blood so I took his place and weighed the filled plastic bags. Chicken parts sped along the conveyor and were then flipped onto designated shoots into sterile plastic bags. But without warning or human intervention the conveyor increased speed dramatically and the flipper missed a chicken giblet which flew straight off the end.

Never did I ever think I would be paid to dive across a concrete floor in order to catch a chicken giblet. I caught the first but didn't make it for the second one, or the rest as they hurtled down the conveyor and onto the floor. A worker slammed the emergency stop button, oblivious to the disconnected wiring, and the conveyor continued to run. With malfunctioning wiring, the automatic flippers refused to flip, the chicken giblets shot off the end, and the Koreans joined me as raw chicken parts were spat across the room. It was only seven in the morning and my day was rapidly spiralling out of control.

As the floor filled with carcasses, I ran to the control panel and ripped out the power supply. The conveyor trundled to a stop, and as the last giblet fell onto the floor, the room fell silent. My breaths were rapid as I scanned the chaos. Body parts were strewn across the bloody floor and all eyes were on me. One of the Koreans knelt down and began picking up the pieces and instinctively we followed suit. While under the conveyor I heard a solid click as the main door opened and from my low vantage point, saw a pair of white boots walk into the room. They looked too big for Nigel, but from the silence that descended the moment they came into the room I knew it was one of the managers. The stillness was broken by a booming voice, echoing from the drab walls, "What the hell is going on here?"

I recognised the voice. It was Bruce, the elusive safety manager. I had already given him a copy of the production report and remembered the dismissive shrug of his shoulders, as he threw it onto his overflowing in-tray. I crawled out from under the conveyor, and stood in front of Bruce, who had his hands held wide in a show of dismay.

"What is going on here, Alistair?" he screamed. "This is against regulations. Clear up that blood and put your hairnet back on." It must have been displaced during my diving catch, but I hadn't realised. As he ranted, I could not help but grin. The whole scene was comical and I had no need to feel incompetent. For six days I had endured the frenzied rush from problem to problem, and witnessed a management team that was clearly inept at running an organisation. All attempts to discuss safety, planning or maintenance had been met with blank looks from all the leaders.

His gaunt cheeks flushed as he barked instructions, but if the desired effect was meant to install fear, the outcome was the opposite. When I finally got the chance to reply. I felt very calm and said quietly, "This room is filled with decent people, who are on their hands and knees scraping blood from the floor because this machine doesn't work properly. As a safety manager you're partly responsible and are putting your workers in danger." He opened his mouth to reply, but I raised my voice to counteract. "As a leader in this organisation you should feel ashamed. The company has no systems, no procedures, and relies on cheap labour to cover up your lack of ability. Either help us clean up this mess, or shut the door on the way out."

I turned my back to him and appealed for help from the workers. The door opened and Bruce retorted, "You're in massive trouble. Massive, I tell you." And then he was gone.

The room was silent for a few seconds and then something strange happened. I got a round of applause, followed by hoots of laughter from the two Australians who had seen and heard every word. One called out, "Alistair, you little ripper. On the upside you're the only person ever to tell him what the whole factory thinks. On the downside he's related to the owner and I'm sorry to say this, but you're history mate."

One of the Asians came over and whispered, "Thank you Mr Alistair, for standing up for us. I have a degree in Industrial Engineering, but they just want me to bag frozen chickens."

I thanked the employee and we went back to work. I knew I would be called away soon, but refused to leave as there was still a production target to make. Two hours later I received an urgent message to go and see Nigel, knowing that it would mean the end of my brief career in chickens. In the safe confines of his office, he attempted a stern face while explaining that my employment contract was no longer valid. I felt a huge sense of relief and held out my hand to thank him, but he couldn't meet my eyes.

As I drove out of the carpark, the owner and his management team stood by the entrance, their arms folded in an act of solidarity. My gut feeling was to wheelspin out of the open gates in a show of machismo. But fresh tyre marks from angry ex-employees were already snaked across the tarmac. There was no need to add any more. I didn't feel anger. I felt sorry for them. This last bastion of management, refusing to improve and ignorant of their actions.

At the factory gate, I stopped the car and walked over to talk with them. The owner reacted uneasily, his feet shuffling as I held out my hand to thank him for the job and the unique experience. He smiled thinly and muttered something about "not being the right fit for the company." After giving farewell handshakes to the rest of his bemused management team, I stopped at Nigel. "Thanks for the job and if you ever find yourself pushing trolleys in the corridor, then do what the American

Indian did in *One Flew Over The Cuckoo's Nest* and jump through the window, then run for your life." He stared at me blankly as I patted him on the shoulder, returned to my car and drove sedately out of the carpark.

Each new challenge in my work life is now compared with those days at the chicken factory. It has become the benchmark whenever I feel that I'm having a bad day. That intense period also made me aware of the skills shortfall that exists within certain sectors of middle management in Australia. Three months after my departure, the factory was put into receivership and now stands empty. It was six months before I could eat chicken again.

12

DREAMTIME

Girl: We're English! English! Do you understand? This is Australia, yes? Where is Adelaide?
White Boy: Ask him for water!
Walkabout Film [1971]
2008. Darwin, Northern Territory.

Under a perfect blue sky, the Qantas 737 touched down in Darwin. It was late November and the flight from Perth had been a relaxed one, with plenty of spare seats and extra servings of in-flight meals. The number of visitors to this part of Australia dwindles between October and December, for one main reason: the build up to the annual rains. It is a time of oppressive heat and high humidity, and visitors that stay too long are prone to going troppo. Spotting someone who's gone troppo is usually quite easy. They are normally white skinned, with a red neck, and no idea where they are heading as they expand useless amounts of energy running around in the midday sun. Think mad dogs, tourists and Englishmen. The locals, it seems, have learnt to adapt and, just like the Spanish, will enjoy long siestas to escape from the humidity.

Darwin is the capital of the Northern Territory, which itself has been unofficially divided into two portions. The upper segment is known as the Top End and encompasses an area of 400,000km. Apart from Darwin, Palmerston and the remote town of Katherine, this vast area is sparsely populated. Most of the land is a wilderness of scrub, grassland and floodplains. In places, you will encounter crocodile infested rivers that carve through steep gorges, millions of years old. From this ancient heartland, the rivers meander across vast flatlands towards the Timor Sea. When it comes to the weather, the main variance throughout the year is the amount of rain. Non-indigenous Australians refer to the Top End as having just two seasons. It is either very wet (the Wet), or extremely dry (the Dry).

Local Aboriginals have different opinions. They observe the subtle moods and characteristics of the landscape, plants and wildlife throughout the year and believe the Northern Territory has six different seasons. According to their natural calendar, we were visiting during a period called *Gunumeleng*. This is the time when the natural world moves at a slower pace and prepares for the torrential rains, which will once again replenish the parched lands.

By the time we touched down in Darwin, the build up to the tropical season had begun. A hazy band of peppered clouds lingered on the distant horizon, and local forecasters were predicting the dried riverbeds would be flowing by Christmas. Vast areas of savannah would then become submerged, blocking off roads and remote communities for months.

The reason for our visit to the Top End during this humid period can be explained. My best friend Steve was planning a whirlwind trip with his family to Singapore and Australia, and they had decided that the Northern Territory was on their wish list. The probability of going troppo or getting drenched in the Wet didn't seem to faze them. This was their only opportunity to experience the Top End and they were prepared to gamble that the rains would hold until their departure. With time in short supply, the plan was simple. Both families would meet in Darwin, then head into Kakadu and Litchfield National Park for a few days. Steve and his family would then continue to Sydney for the next leg of their tour.

We were the first to arrive in Darwin and had booked both families into a family run motel along the tourist strip. All we needed now was a taxi to get us there. As we waited in air-conditioned comfort for our luggage to canter along the conveyer, I received a text message from Steve and his wife, Mel. At that moment, they were lounging by their hotel pool, enjoying a Singapore Sling before heading to Changi airport. It had been years since we had last met, and I found myself grinning excitedly as we collected our luggage and headed towards the exit. Fran was in full stride, and our two children ran alongside the luggage trolley, eager to set foot in the Northern Territory.

The automatic doors opened to reveal a burst of bright sunshine, and we waltzed full gallop into a veil of air, so warm and clammy, each of us momentarily stopped in our tracks. It was only a short stroll to the taxi rank, but the humidity acted like treacle and, after a few more steps, my youngest boy, Seby, cradled his mums legs and cried out, "Mummy, please. I'm hot and thirsty." She looked over at me, but I didn't respond. If we couldn't make it to the taxi rank without crumbling, what type of adventure-family were we? The oldest boy, Noah, decided he was also suffering and called out, "Daddy, water please."

A pedestrian glanced over as I whispered, "We've just spent three hours on a flight and during that time we were all wined, dined, fed, watered and entertained. The taxi rank is just over there. I'm sure we can all make it without dehydrating." Noah turned towards his mum and repeated the words, hoping to receive a compassionate reply. Our boys were very young, just two years and four, so I should have been far more sympathetic and felt a surge of guilt as we joined the taxi queue. Fran left me to ponder my actions, taking the children in search of bottled water as I watched over our luggage.

I didn't want to admit I now regretted getting into the holiday mood by enjoying several beers during the flight. A dull ache was forming deep within my skull, and my parched lips craved water. It didn't help that the designer of Darwin airport had decided to install tin cladding on the terminal walls, which may have won him an award for art, but created a cauldron for those sweltering in the taxi rank.

Our driver was a thickset, heavily bearded man of few words. As we drove away, he mumbled about the mild temperatures and lack of rain clouds. What he lacked in conversation he made up for with a fully functional air conditioner that blasted cool air across the interior. In blissful silence, we sped through Darwin's outer suburbs towards the thought of a welcome dip in the pool, followed by a refreshing shower.

The online image of the tropical pool, lined with palm trees, turned out to be a small plunge pool hidden behind a metal-railed fence. The water was milky green and felt warm enough to bathe in. All it required was bubbles. The "cosmopolitan mix of overseas travellers", booked into the motel, looked to be migrant families in transit from war town countries, and the "neat and pleasant accommodation" was a sparsely furnished, one bedroomed prison. As I pulled open the stiff curtains, a sliver of light shone across the pale blue walls. They were lined with thin cracks, creeping from the ceiling, across the width of the room and down towards the fake timber floor.

In an effort to alleviate the clammy air, an overhead fan, controlled by two speeds, ventilated our room. The first speed was a gentle whirr that did little to quell the stifling heat trapped inside the four walls. The second speed was much more exciting. The solitary light bulb dimmed as the fan quickly picked up speed and revved towards maximum revolutions, its wide blades swishing noisily through the warm air.

To escape the mugginess, Fran took the boys to the pool, while I opted for an afternoon walk to investigate a hired car franchise, which according to the friendly motel receptionist, was a few blocks away. As I entered the corridor, Fran passed me a small water bottle and advised, "Don't forget your baseball cap!" With a spring in my step, I called out, "I'll be ok. It's just down the road, and the brief walk will clear my head."

I stepped into bright sunshine and was instantly transported to a world devoid of pedestrians. While traversing the empty pavements, drivers glanced over and then quickly returned their stare to the road ahead. Where possible, I stayed close to buildings, to take advantage of a thin strip of shadow, and then studied the colourful tourist map handed over by the receptionist. The scale was inaccurate, and it was clear that the journey would take longer than envisaged, with many roads to cross.

While waiting impatiently at an intersection for traffic lights to change, I drained the water bottle, savouring each and every precious drop. With the bottle empty, I refocused my attention, to find the traffic had stopped and the little green man on the opposite side of the road was flashing.

Two rows of cars were lined up behind a faded white line, revving impatiently as I ambled past. Each vehicle was cocooned, their tinted windows closed, with just one person inside. All drivers wore sunglasses and stared straight ahead, in air-conditioned nirvana, as I ventured past under a radiant sky.

After circumnavigating three more sets of traffic lights, I finally located the car hire franchise, and as I entered, an arctic wind from the wall mounted air conditioner whipped across my sweaty scalp. I stopped momentarily, wiped my brow and gathered my senses. In the space of three steps, the temperature had dropped from an oppressive 42 degrees to a seemingly chilly 20. I inhaled deeply on the cool, artificial air and strode purposely to the front counter. A dark haired girl, smartly dressed in a bright blue jacket and matching skirt, sat behind a low counter, in readiness for a customer. When I approached, she looked up from her computer, smiled brightly and said, "G'day mate. How can I help?"

"Water please!" were the first words that slipped out of my parched mouth. She understood. Without a word, she revolved 180 degrees on her office chair, walked into another room and returned with a tall glass, filled with chilled water. I emptied the glass in one go, but let pride get in the way of requesting a top up. As my throat eased, I smiled and said thanks, hoping I now looked capable of striking a good deal. She then asked, "Did you walk here, mate?" I nodded and replied, "I thought the afternoon stroll would do me good after the long flight from Perth."

She giggled and retorted, "Most visitors jump in the hotel pool as soon as they arrive and then call us from their mobile after they've cooled down. People rarely walk far these days. Are you English?"

During the trek back to the hostel, the late afternoon sun continued its onslaught on my exposed scalp, and once again, cars proved they ruled over pedestrians. At each junction they raced past, oblivious to a solitary pedestrian leaning against the traffic light pole, waiting for the flashing green man to help him cross.

Hours after leaving the hostel, I staggered into my room and collapsed onto the bed. The build up to the holiday had been frantic, with too many overtime hours and not enough sleep. I had finally hit the wall. Within minutes, I was sucked into a hazy dream, oblivious to the mechanical whirr of the overhead fan, and dreamt about little green men calling me to join them as they frolicked in a sparkling pool. I woke sluggishly to the distant sound of helicopter blades and had a hazy flashback to Martin Sheen in *Apocalypse Now*. Just like him, I felt dazed, hung over and confused. Maybe I was already going troppo!

Suddenly the door burst open and the room was

flooded by bright light from the corridor. I sat upright, just as Fran and the boys came into view, refreshed and excited after their time in the pool. Noah took one look at me, toddled over and said, "Daddy, why are you in bed? The pool was fun."

Steve and his family touched down after midnight, after enjoying a few days at a luxurious stopover resort. I remained awake until their arrival, keen to rekindle a friendship that had been teetering on the brink. Steve's parting words, when I moved from England to Australia, had stayed with me for years. "I don't do virtual friends very well. I like people I can visit without getting a visa! Australia is a long way away, so don't expect a visit anytime soon." That had been three years prior, and now he was here with his family.

Steve had always been abrupt. I loved this attribute and his total honesty. I missed his quirky viewpoints and infectious laughter. I was godfather to his oldest daughter, Molly, but had rarely been in touch. What kind of role model was I? Mel would forgive me. Wouldn't she? We had always been good friends, since Steve had started dating her, and I had been thrilled to be their best man. But I was becoming a stranger now. To Molly and Daisy, I was more of a name than a real person, my faded image ignored as they walked past their parents wedding photo each morning. I could imagine the conversation on the flight to Australia as Mel explained where the girls were going.

Mel: "So girls, don't forget to be polite to Uncle Ali and Aunty Fran."

Daisy: "Is Uncle Ali, really our Uncle?"

Mel: "Well no, but —"

Molly: "Why did he move to Australia with Aunty Fran?"

Mel: "Well we don't know really but maybe we'll find out —"

Daisy: "Have they got a pet kangaroo?"

Mel: "No, Daisy. We probably won't see any kangaroos unless we go to a wildlife park. They haven't got any pets, as far as—"

Daisy: "Is he still bald?"

Mel: "I guess so, and probably more wrinkled than last time we met."

Daisy: "Is Daddy still his friend?"

Mel: "Yes, my poppet. But Daddy hasn't seen him in a few years, so it might be a bit emotional when they meet."

Molly: "Does Uncle Ali still think he's funny?"

Mel: "I guess so, dear. Some things never change. Now let's settle down and finish the movie. We've started to descend."

By now, I had reverted to the thinnest clothes I could muster and was waiting in the hotel foyer, dressed in a singlet and running shorts. I was barefoot, sunburnt, unshaven, and in need of a rest. Overnight, I had turned from a sanely dressed suburbanite into a Top End Bogan.

I must have nodded off by the unmanned reception desk, as I didn't hear their taxi arrive. They lumbered noisily through the doorway, carting a multitude of matching suitcases and then stood silently in the entrance as I rose to greet them. As my eyes adjusted to the musky light, I felt a rush of emotions along with a multitude of obscure thoughts. Why were they all wearing long trousers and walking boots? Why had they bought so much luggage for a four week holiday? How had the girls managed to grow so quickly in three years? Why had I booked such a crappy motel? Why hadn't Steve and Mel aged in the years since we last met? Why were they all staring at me?

As Steve sidestepped a discarded daypack, he shook my outstretched hand and announced, "The Australian lifestyle seems to suit you. I see you've dressed up for the occasion and know all the top hotels in Darwin." Mel smiled weakly, and their two young girls sat down on the floor, oblivious to my requests for high fives, begging instead for water and a bed!

While the children slept, mosquitos blitzed the outer fringes of the room, unable to penetrate the thermal shock waves from the overhead fan. The four adults sat quietly in the cool passageway, and as beers flowed, we reminisced about the past and caught up on gossip. Steve and I had previously enjoyed many adventures together and had always hoped our children would become best friends and share escapades. We were now together, in the Top End of Australia, finally taking steps to make that happen.

After a day in Darwin to experience the local sights, we collected the hired cars at first light and then headed into the interior. The children soon became inseparable, as were Fran and Mel, who shared one car while Steve and I took the other. Kakadu National Park is tantalisingly close to Darwin and within minutes of leaving the outer suburbs, the urban landscape gave way to disused scrubland and red dirt. With just one sealed road to follow, and very few cars to think about, the morning drifted past as we sped into the shimmering distance.

A road sign depicted the bold outline of a kangaroo and informed us giant termites were nearby, so we pulled over to investigate. Apart from the bush flies, which seemed to have been waiting for fresh tourists and buzzed incessantly around our faces, there was no trace of kangaroos. Nearby, were a series of natural monoliths, many over two metres tall and home to armies of termites. The ochre linings of each mound were pitted and battled-scarred due to the onslaught from the extreme elements, but deep inside, the termites were protected.

To insulate themselves from the stifling heat, termites construct living chambers interlinked with vertical ventilation shafts, which create a natural air conditioner. Regardless of the outside temperature, this feat of engineering cools the core to a liveable, constant temperature of 30 degrees Celsius.

As soon as we parked, the children escaped and ran across the parched savannah to investigate. While bounding across the red dirt, they ignored the barrage of questions and instructions from their concerned mothers. "Molly, goodness me, watch out for snakes;" "Noah, put your shoes on;" "Daisy, don't you dare touch anything!" "Girls, have you put on sun screen?" and "Seby, wait there for me. Where's your hat gone?"

After surviving the termite mounds, the remainder of the morning's journey proved uneventful as we sped through a semi wilderness towards the heart of Kakadu. By lunchtime, we were booked into a tourist park, complete with neat cabins, a sparkling pool and an onsite restaurant.

"Look, Daddy, a frog." Seby called out, as we played together in the shallow end of the pool. He climbed onto my back, and I swam nearer to investigate. The reptile was nearly as wide as my hand, with tiny warts on its dappled back, and I had a good idea this was our first encounter with a cane toad. In 1935, the Bureau of Sugar Experiments introduced cane toads into Queensland from Hawaii, in an experiment to help control the native grey backed sugar cane beetle. There is no doubt the toads enjoy munching sugar cane beetles and have eaten thousands, if not millions of them. But the story doesn't end there.

Cane toads are extremely toxic, and Australian predators are not adapted to cope with ingesting the poisonous glands that protrude from their skin. They may look tasty to eat, but there has been a massive reduction in goanna and snake populations in areas inhabited by cane toads. There is worse news to come. They have a natural tendency to travel and have now hopped across Queensland, New South Wales and many parts of the Northern Territory. They now number 200 million and are seemingly unstoppable as they continue to impact on the unique Australian eco-system and migrate further west and south. As for the native grey backed beetle, they are still a pest, but the Bureau of Sugar Experiments is unusually quiet these days.

I picked up the toad by one of its meaty legs, and together with Seby, we walked across the manicured lawn towards the nearby restaurant, where a few workers were enjoying cool drinks before dinner. While crossing the floor, I called out, "Excuse me, but my young lad found this in the pool. I think it's a cane toad."

Their conversation ceased as they studied the warty creature, dangling between my fingertips. One man stood, adjusted his wide brimmed hat and came closer to investigate. He had piercing blue eyes, weathered skin and the steady gait of someone in charge. As he approached, he took one look at the reptile and said in a slow drawl, "Yes, mate. That's a cane toad. Well spotted." He then kneeled down, looked directly at Seby and whispered, "Do you like Australian wildlife, young'un?"

Seby nodded, but was unusually muted, and squeezed my free hand with his. The man rustled Seby's fair hair, stood upright, took the toad and said clearly, "Well I'm glad, and so do I. This here is a cane toad and in Kakadu we hate them with a vengeance. They kill our wildlife and, with a destructive creature like this, there's just one thing to do. Now close your eyes if you don't like blood."

He then hurled the toad against a timber door with such ferocity that it splattered hard, bounced onto the floor and lay perfectly still. As the man returned to his drink, he turned his face back towards us and explained, "If you see any more of those damn things, feel free to do the same."

Seby couldn't wait to tell the other children about the new game of cane toad bashing, and the rest of the afternoon was spent searching for them in the confines of the lawn and pool area. A bounty was given for each one, and a few hours later, Australia only had 199,999,997 left to exterminate.

The following morning, we drove to the small community of Yellow Waters and spent a few lazy hours cruising along a tributary of the South Alligator River in search of wildlife. The area is Kakadu's largest river system, where billabongs, floodplains and swamps merge to create a vast aquatic wilderness.

The river guide's number one rule was crucial: keep all body parts in the boat at all times unless you want to be chomped by a croc! As we glided through the pristine waters, spotting crocs, from the safety of the boat, became an easy pastime. Some floated near the edge of the river, lying perfectly still, with just their steely eyes and speckled nose showing above the waterline, but most basked in the sunshine along the riverbank. Overhead, magpie geese and whistling ducks flew in formation, while great egrets foraged in the shallow waters, probing for food amongst a carpet of blue lilies.

With the boat tour over, it was time to track down our Aboriginal guide, Patsy. She collaborates with a travel organisation called Animal Tracks, to take visitors on a tour of her tribal land, and shares an abundance of knowledge about bush tucker and the environment. *Bush Tucker* is the term that Australians use for food found in the wild. Bush means wilderness and Tucker is Australian slang for food.

My hope was the experience would give Steve and his family a lasting impression of the *real Australia* and an insight to why we now called Australia home. We had been lucky. By late November, extreme humidity, high temperatures and the chance of flash flooding would normally curtail this type of activity. But the heat was bearable, and the clouds were still playing hide and seek.

At midday we met Rachael, the representative from Animal Tracks, and after brief introductions with other passengers, we boarded a four-wheel drive truck and headed into the bush to meet Patsy. Rachael was previously a Kakadu park ranger and immediately formed a strong connection with the group as she passionately explained the afternoon's itinerary and the ecological importance of the wetlands to Australia and the world. She also took time to explain Patsy was a traditional owner of the land and had been living in the Northern Territories all her life, often nomadically, and was one of the last remaining hunter-gatherers left in Australia.

With the talking over, the truck headed into the bush, along dirt roads, towards Patsy's land. She was waiting by the side of the road, dressed in a long skirt, matching top and a pair of training shoes and joined Rachael up front, turning round to greet us as she hopped on board. Her hair was a wild frizz of golden yellow and her dark skin had a healthy glow, as though it was perfectly adapted to life under the sun. As Rachael headed into the interior,

Patsy joined her in small talk while the passenger's glugged on water and exchanged travel stories within the close confines of the rear seats.

When we disembarked, I took a few steps away from the excited children and stole a quick look at Patsy's homeland. The surrounding area was teeming with birds and insects. The air crackled with the sound of droning mosquitos and, in the nearby trees, flocks of noisy waterbirds sheltered from the searing rays of the sun. The grassland nearby was firm, but in the distance, isolated areas were covered in a thin veneer of still water, fringed by blue lilies and colourful wildflowers.

Patsy emerged from the rear of the truck and handed each of us a wooden stick. As the group fell silent, she explained, "This is used for locating the turtles, as they are lying under the ground to escape the heat. Watch me first and you will learn quickly." The children were wide eyed as she strode across the meadow, then found a suitable location at the base of a paperbark tree and began probing the soft ground. We all followed swiftly, eager to learn for ourselves.

Hunting for turtles

How she did it so quickly I don't know, but after a few attempts she called us over and said. "Quiet, please. I will show you once more." As she prodded the stick into the mud, the muted sound of a submerged shell could just be heard. She then bent down, plunged her hands and arms into the moist earth and scooped out a long necked turtle. The waking creature looked slightly bemused at all the attention, but was stuffed into a hessian bag and Patsy urged us to continue.

The children ran towards the boggiest patch and were soon plastered in a sheen of black mud as they noisily searched for their dinner. Within thirty minutes, the group had located two more turtles and Patsy called a halt. "That is enough." she announced, with quiet authority. "We must only take what we need."

Rachael and Patsy worked well together, and as we traversed the landscape, stopping to forage for herbs and paperbark, they enthusiastically informed us about the abundance of bush food available in the region. Patsy had already caught and killed two magpie geese before we had picked her up. They were now in the hessian bag, waiting to be plucked. Bush Tucker skills are becoming rare, as Aboriginals abandon their traditional way of life. Most have adapted a hybrid lifestyle, where they still live together in large family communities, but crave western world indulgences. Indigenous populations across the world have struggled when faced with this type of cultural change, and Aboriginals are no different.

Our final jaunt was a hunt for file snakes in a small billabong at the edge of the reserve. These aquatic snakes struggle to move on land and as Patsy plucked a metre long reptile from the water, she threw it onto the grass where it sluggishly languished on the bank.

She turned to the group and asked, "OK. I need a volunteer to help me prepare the snake."

Fran's hand shot up and she called out, "Yes I'll do it."

Patsy picked up the thin snake by its tail and explained. "No worries. All you do is take the head in your mouth and crunch down hard."

Fran's hand dropped, but she moved forward to collect the snake and asked, "I might try, but is it poisonous?"

"No, lady. Don't worry. I will show you how it's done. But before I kill the snake, I have one question for you all. Do we have enough food already?"

The group went quiet, but from the edge of the billabong, Molly called out, "I think we have plenty already, so please let it go." There was a murmur of agreement and with that, Patsy gently dropped the snake into the water and declared the hunting over! The sun had now lost its edge, and harsh light was now replaced by a soft radiance, which brushed the treetops and turned the grassland into a sea of rippling amber.

During the final hour of daylight, a bonfire was lit, and while preparing for dinner, a herd of wild buffalo appeared from the bush. They roamed silently across the adjoining paddock, skirted a band of woodland and then melted into the deepening shadows. As they crossed our line of sight, Patsy pulled one of the turtles from her bag and handed it to Steve. He stood for a moment, unsure of what do, and caressed its long neck while his family watched. It was a classic setting, with the sun dropping low on the horizon, outlining the wide horns of wild buffalos on the savannah.

Patsy broke the serenity by asking out loud, "You gonna stroke it or kill it, mister? Your family are hungry. Break its neck so we can roast it!" As Steve grappled with the wriggling creature, his two children looked on in awe. They were now smeared in goblets of dried mud, and throughout the afternoon, hadn't complained once about the heat, mosquitos or lack of toilets.

Two days earlier, Mel had been sipping cocktails in Singapore. Now she was sitting on the red dirt, humming a Scottish ballad, while plucking feathers from dead geese. At the edge of camp, Noah and Seby were enjoying spear-throwing lessons from Rachael, while Fran prepared fresh herbs for dinner.

The seasoned meat was then covered in paperbark and roasted along the edge of the fireplace. Nothing was wasted, as we silently devoured the succulent geese, turtle and sweet potatoes. With dinner complete, Patsy promised a nutritional dessert and led us to a line of paperbark trees at the edge of camp. Each of their trunks was swarming with ants, and according to Patsy, this species were nutritional and delicious. She swiped her hand across a tree trunk, gathering enough ants to make a small black morsel and popped it into her mouth. As she bit down, she smiled and said, "Just like lemons. Now you try."

The children were keen, picking off ants between fits of giggles, as the tiny insects crawled across fingers, hands and faces. The trick was to collect enough to create a slightly crushed ball, to ensure you had no rogue ants roaming alone in your mouth. Each morsel delivered a sharp burst of zingy lemon, high in vitamin C and instantly addictive.

From faraway, Rachael announced it was time to leave, and as we headed towards the truck, I realised that Noah was missing. I quickly scanned the distant buffalo for signs of activity, then ran towards the dampened fireplace and searched the camp. Fran had already located him and called me over to watch his activities. He had returned for more dessert and was standing by a tree trunk, talking softly to himself while picking off ants. His blonde curly hair was matted with mud and his clothes were now unrecognisable, but he, like all the visitors, had learnt so much in one short day.

Far on the horizon, new clouds were forming; their wispy edges blushed from the setting sun as they spread low across the savannah. As the weary group reluctantly boarded the truck for the return journey, I heard Patsy whisper to Rachael, "It is time, my friend. The rains are approaching, and I think this will be our final week of the season."

Within 48 hours, Steve and his family departed for Sydney. The skies above Darwin airport were dark and foreboding and I watched from the departure lounge as swirling clouds swallowed their plane. They were now in search of their next adventure and would soon be climbing the Sydney Harbour Bridge, visiting family and taking surf lessons at Bondi Beach. Our flight was due soon, towards the south, in readiness for summer.

Two weeks later, they arrived at our front door and we finally had them to ourselves. They had woken that morning on the east coast, flown across the country, hired a car and were now in the south west of Australia. After a hectic few weeks, my fears had come true. They looked exhausted.

While they had been gallivanting, Fran and I had planned a plethora of day trips to show off our part of the world and to give them an insight into our daily lives. The house had been scrubbed, the garage fumigated and the alfresco area decorated in preparation for their arrival. Friends had been booked, barbeques organised and the weatherman had confirmed a week of unbroken sunshine. The beer fridge brimmed with fresh juices for the girls, zingy bottles of Shiraz for Mel and locally brewed ales for Steve. We were ready to enjoy balmy evenings under the stars, listen to their Australian adventures and share funny stories with the children.

While giving them an impromptu house tour and pointing out the usual features, such as the mosquito spray, fly swatter and stash of Doritos, Steve was unusually quiet. The girls had disappeared, running off with the boys to check out the bunk beds, while Fran and Mel were already comparing décor and sipping wine.

I led Steve into the back garden, hoping he would comment on the decking area, recently oiled and now decorated with an array of tropical plants stuffed into terracotta pots. The white washed walls were lined with intimate knick-knacks from global travels, including an abstract mural from darkest Peru and a tribal mask from Indonesia. Pride of place was a framed photo of Steve and I, clad in thick fleeces, ski masks, and proudly holding up ice axes. We were standing on the summit of Mount Blanc, the highest mountain in Western Europe.

But he brushed past the artefacts without a second glance, his eyes locking onto our striped hammock, gently swaying in the warm summer breeze. He dropped his daypack onto the grass, kicked off his sandals and eased into the hammock, sighing softly as his long legs curled around the sides. For a few seconds there was silence, and then he said softly, "I know you'll have heaps of things planned for us. Wineries I'm guessing, and deep sea fishing plus a chance to meet your new mates."

I had the itinerary folded neatly in my pocket, ready to show him, but something told me to keep it there. "To tell you the truth," he began. "We're worn out from travelling. All I want to do all week is laze in this hammock, take walks on your local beach and enjoy a cold beer each evening. Nothing more. I've seen every alcove and beach in Sydney, but we always seemed to be driving past them, not lying on them. I need to stop. I'm sure the wineries are amazing, the deep-sea fishing is fantastic and your mates are nice people. But I'm tired of moving."

I understood exactly. Australia is a massive country, and too many travellers try and skim across vast distances in short time in an effort to experience the main sights. I left him swaying, grabbed two cold beers from the fridge and threw the itinerary in the bin.

Their last days in Australia were relaxed and simplistic. Hammock time was in. Long car journeys were out. Whenever a venture was discussed that warranted a trip in the car, the same question would come up. "How long will we be, and is it better than lounging in the hammock or enjoying the local beach?"

We talked a lot. About dreams, aspirations, future travels, and coming to terms with living 19 hours flight time from best friends. We made plans to stay in touch, to use Skype and be virtual friends! He complimented us on the decking, and they all appreciated the rural outlook from our front veranda, where eagles soared on midday thermals and kangaroos hopped each evening under a burning sky.

On their final morning, I launched my small aluminium boat into the clear, pristine waters of Geographe Bay. The ocean was eerily flat, merging with the distant horizon, and the sun was still low enough to warrant extra layers. All morning we explored the bay, fishing in secret spots for herring, skipjack and squid. Mel and the girls cast crab pots into the water, and then shrieked with delight as they pulled two large crustaceans from the depths, their bright blue pincers gnashing in defence. The rules for crabbing are easy to follow. If you catch a pregnant female, you drop her back into the water. If you catch an undersize male, you do the same. The bag limit is 10 crabs per person, but we were never in danger of finding so many.

The rising sun stirred the bay, and sailboats appeared, their ivory sails dotted across the shimmering waters. Overhead, fluffy clouds floated past, casting tiny shadows across the bay as the boat rocked gently in the increasing swell. Our catch had been meagre. But no one cared. We had enough to prepare chilli crab, grilled squid and a taster of fresh herring. It was time to head home for our final barbeque.

As I throttled the outboard, the boat changed pitch and skimmed easily across the water. Steve lay upfront, tanned and relaxed, his long arms dangling loosely over the sides. We sped across the bay, past a lone kayaker and small fishing boats then headed towards the town jetty, a 1.8km wooden structure that juts proudly into the Indian Ocean. Fishermen were lined along its length, so I turned the tiller sedately, and for a few seconds, we sped parallel with the jetty and aimed for land.

Just off our bow, a dolphin surfaced briefly, its dorsal fin carving easily through the water, and within seconds it was gone. As the beach drew nearer, I eased off the revs and the boat slowed. Steve turned his face from the water and glanced over towards me, his face a beaming smile. The engine noise was low now, just a gentle chug, and as the hull skimmed the sand, he called out, "I get it. On a day like today, I get it."

13

LONG HOT SUMMER

> "Every summer has its own story."
> **Unknown**

2010. Western Australia

Australia has sunshine in abundance, but their summers are different. They refuse to budge. Week after week of deep blue skies sounds idyllic and in many ways it is. You learn to get up early on the weekend to take your morning swim. You watch the locals water their lawns by hosepipe every sunset, with a beer in hand and a friendly wave. Adverts on the radio warn listeners to avoid the sun between mid-morning and mid-afternoon, due to cancerous UV rays beating down from the sun.

It's all about preparation. Gardeners check their automatic sprinklers are in good working order and set their time clocks for the two allocated days set down by the local council, unless you water by hand with a hosepipe. Boat owners wash the winter grime from their hulls, evict spiders from outboard engines and locate abandoned crab nets from behind their backyard sheds.

The main event was my brother Dave coming to visit as part of his world tour. We have two young children and no matter how hard I try and tell them that they have family on the other side of the world, it's sometimes difficult for them to understand. They were still young, just four and six and very excited about meeting Uncle Dave as he flew in from South America. Despite the long air journey he was chirpy and instantly at ease with his nephews. His shaved head was deeply tanned and the adventure had toned his fifty-something body. As we drove home, the boys sat either side of him, listening to every word of his jungle escapades and I felt very proud as he handed out gifts and recited tall stories.

With Dave visiting, summer was a magical time and now that he has returned to the UK, I took time to reminisce about the special times that we had. He insisted on cooking Christmas breakfast on the barbeque and our two boys stood by his side the whole time, helping him prepare the banquet. Each weekend we would cycle to my local pub for a beer and during one of those happy hours, we got chatting with some locals.

"Would you live here, Dave?" one of them asked.

"No, it's too quiet for me." was his honest answer.

The wide-eyed look said it all and the local probed further, "How can Australia be perceived as quiet?" Dave put down his beer and answered with a straight face, "I can see why Alistair and Fran are here. It's great for their children and there's plenty of sunshine. But I crave diversity without travelling hours by plane. I love climbing in Scotland, skiing in Chamonix, nights out in London, going to the pub with mates I have known all my life, watching real football and to be truthful, the long, hot summers would drive me crazy."

I knew that Australia had snow-clad mountain ranges, held major sporting events and had numerous cosmopolitan cities. It was just the large distances between them that seemed to irk Dave.

As much as we all wanted him to stay longer, he's filled with a sense of wanderlust and craves faraway places. On his final night, we grabbed a few beers and cycled down to the beach to watch the sunset. It was a balmy evening and the water's edge was alive with children splashing, dogs paddling and fisherman casting their lines into the calm bay.

Paddle boarder on Geographe Bay, Busselton.

Our Australian summer
And so it is
I stay and you leave
On a flight to London, and friends
A lone paddle boarder glides past
As the sun slides
Big sky, melting
A warm breeze stirs the shore
And we reach for T-shirts
Then sip cold beer
And reminisce
About childhood and Mum
Summer is ending
And the plane will be waiting
Each evening
You watered the lawn
And waved to the neighbours
With beer in hand
Pale skin at first
Then pink
Now tanned
We fished at dawn
You were the anchor man
The big five we called them
Herring and squid
And three more that we had never seen
In fishing magazines
These went back
But not the squid
Or the herring
Sunset barbeques
With neighbours
As they listened to your stories

About mountains and jungles
Six weeks of summer and no TV
You enjoyed the hammock
Swaying in the breeze
With our boys
Embraced
Telling travel stories
About trekking and scuba diving
They chuckled
And sat close, eyes wide
You drank tea and told jokes
Before dinner
You picked tomatoes
Every day so many
In our small patch
Now neglected
The leaves shriveled
The flies have gone, thankfully
They got silly
Too many, too crazy
It's the end of summer
And now we are here
Watching the bay
And the paddle boarder glides past
Oblivious
Tomorrow you are gone
No more treats for the boys
From their Uncle
No more ice creams
Or fizzy drinks
Or silly jokes
It's the end of summer
Of time with my brother

There were tears at the airport. Our boys had enjoyed having an Uncle in the house. We appreciated someone treating them special, as only family know how. But there are too many other countries in the world for Dave to explore and I knew he wouldn't be back to Australia for a few years at least. His nephews will remember his jokes and antics for some time, but they will grow considerably before they next meet Uncle Dave. I hope it's not too long. They are only children for a short period and deserve to be spoilt by uncles and aunties.

Maybe it's our turn to travel home, before they forget about their family half a world away. Skype helps and so does FaceTime. But virtual interactions don't lead to ice cream and tickles. According to the BBC there is talk of an El Nino weather pattern forming in the northern hemisphere which could lead to a long, hot summer across the UK. It seems like a perfect reason for us to visit Uncle Dave.

14

SUNRISE

"Once a year go someplace you've never been before."
Dalai Lama
2012. Albany, Western Australia.

In the UK, my camping trips consisted of summer weekends in the Lake District with friends. Life was simple then. A two-man tent, a Millets sleeping bag and a torch. The local pub at Dungeon Ghyll served evening meals and after ten miles hiking, followed by a few pints of Old Peculiar, the wind and rain were forgotten as I slept soundly in the tent alongside my best friend, Steve.

Camping in Australia is big business. During spring and summer it has a perfect climate for outdoor living. Families embrace the lifestyle and with guaranteed sunshine, booking a camping holiday is not the lottery that you get in other countries. Retirees spend their children's inheritance following the sun and circumnavigating the country as the seasons change. They are known as Grey

Nomads and tow their caravans to many destinations across the vast country. From November until April, the Grey Nomads spend time in the southern half of the country to avoid the monsoonal rains (*The Wet*) in the north.

Since moving Down Under we have invested in a camper trailer and one Christmas we joined the Grey Nomads and throngs of excited families as they joined together in a coastal camping park in Albany, Western Australia. During our trip, I wrote the following article, which was subsequently published in a national newspaper called The Weekend West:

Amazing Albany

Up until last week my family had never experienced a summer holiday in Albany, so a Christmas camping trip was planned in order to experience this historical and diverse part of the 'Great Southern' region. As our car entered the town, a proud signpost declared we were in "Amazing Albany." It was amazingly hot, but still cooler than the stifled streets of Perth, and the campsite was filled with holidaymakers who had fled south in search of respite from the Christmas heatwave.

After setting up our home, we made contact with our neighbours and were invited for sundowners by a family of four from Perth. There is something about camping that seems to reconnect people. With no TV, children use their imaginations rather than the remote control and make friends instantly. Adults seem to make more effort too and as we enjoyed drinks with our new friends, the children played in the park and fishermen ambled past on their way to the beach.

Just after 6am the following morning, I crawled out of our camper trailer and greeted the rising sun. I could see that I was not the only early riser, with excited children already playing in the park, serenaded by dads drinking their first coffee of the day. I grabbed my camera and wallet and decided to embrace the early morning by heading to the beach. The faint smell of sizzling bacon lingered in the warm breeze as I weaved through rows of multicoloured tents and overland caravans towards the nearby dunes that led to the foreshore.

Middleton beach was perfect. No people, no footprints and no sound, except the gentle lapping of water as it broke on the shoreline. Two container ships were moored in the deep channel of King George Sound and a solitary fishing boat chugged past, en route to a secret spot, no doubt. I removed my sandals, feeling the need to feel sand between my toes and as I walked, a faint squeak could be heard with every imprint. Then I remembered a conversation I had overheard at the camp barbeque the previous evening, about Middleton beach being so pristine that the sand squeaks. At the time I thought it was just another campfire fable, but here I was, walking and squeaking, just as they had mentioned.

I turned left, passing two small natural coves where early bathers swam silently in the calm waters. I left my sandals on the beach and edged into the water so that it lapped gently to my knees. It wasn't as chilly as I expected the Southern Ocean to be. For a few seconds I contemplated a swim. But there was still much to explore so I waded back and continued my exploration of the coast.

I left the cove and headed to Emu Point for my first glimpse of Oyster Harbour, a wide turquoise inlet surrounded by an amphitheatre of wooded hills. The water glistened in the early morning light and pelicans appeared on the horizon, gliding inches from the flat water, before skidding to a stop in the shallows. The tide was out, allowing two fishermen to walk into the bay. They were 200 metres off shore, standing knee deep as they cast into the bright water. A lone pelican paddled close by eager to share their catch of the day, and I also went in search of food.

By now it was 7.30am and Emu Point Café had opened. Perched at the end of a quiet road it has panoramic views of the expansive inlet and sits tantalisingly close to the golden sands that recently won the award for cleanest beach in Western Australia. As I ordered breakfast, early morning cyclists appeared at the counter followed by an unshaven camper who ambled in for a newspaper and fresh coffee. I sipped a cappuccino and gazed over the azure waters to the fishermen and optimistic pelican.

The first paddle boarder arrived at 8am, skimming across the flat water towards the floating jetty and was joined by a lone swimmer as the sun gained strength and climbed steadily in the clear blue sky. The manicured park was still relatively quiet, but the mercury was rising and those sleeping in tents would soon be forced awake by heat and light. Very soon the early morning ambience would be lost. My breakfast arrived with a smile and I took one more look at Oyster Bay as it wakened. I hope the fishermen shared one of their fish with the pelican. I didn't share my eggs benedict with anyone. They were too delicious. I had only been in Albany one night and it already felt amazing.

15

THE BRIDGE

"I do love cricket. It's so very English."
Sarah Bernhardt
2013. Sydney, Western Australia

Sydney is a dream location to visit, so when the opportunity came to travel from Perth to watch the final test cricket match, I didn't need too much convincing. I hadn't envisaged that the England cricket team would be 4-0 down by the time I reached Sydney, but as the taxi dropped my friends and me outside the historic stadium, there was little evidence from the carnival atmosphere that a whitewash was looming.

Bright sunshine forced us to abandon our seats in favour of the spectators' bar and while queuing for refreshments I joined in with the banter as Australians and English traded verbal punches. From afar I could see a mass of red and white that could only be the Barmy

Army supporters and throughout the day they sang stirring tunes from England's historic past.

In recent years the Australians have formed their own army of dedicated spectators called The Fanatics and during the game they sat close to the Barmy Army. Some fanatics wore Mexican hats and others were dressed in bright yellow shirts. But most seemed happy to wear the traditional Aussie attire of knee-length shorts and cheap cotton singlet's. English supporters have been raised on the football terraces, and opposing fans expect a tirade of verbal abuse when their team loses. Despite Australia's epic performance, their supporters were unusually quiet. There were a few sporadic instances where The Fanatics came to their feet and hollered across the terrace, informing the English supporters at how pathetic they were at cricket. The result was always the same. A few seconds of silence and then the Barmy Army supporters would reply with the stirring chorus of "The Mighty Mighty England."

From my vantage point by the bar, it was clear that there was nothing mighty about this particular English cricket team and as the days unfolded, I began to think about all the iconic tourist sites in Sydney that I was missing out on. Throughout the first days I chatted constantly with fellow Brits as they watched from the shade, or stood in line for more beer. Many had made the long haul flight from England and this was their trip of a lifetime, regardless of the result. Others had travelled interstate, with Australia now their new home. As the conversations flowed, I realised that those who had migrated were the ones most likely to be wearing football or rugby shirts from their home town back in the UK. I understood why. It's about feeling part of something, regardless of the fact that you now live on the other side of the world.

Sydney seemed to be the hottest destination for those on a two-year working visa and the young British I spoke with were lapping up the experience of living half a world away. For three nights the trendy back streets had reverberated with lively chants as the overseas supporters staked their claim to quayside bars, seemingly oblivious to the fact that a five-nil defeat was looming. But the continuing sight of England's demise on the hallowed turf finally became too painful for me to endure, especially as there was so much more to see in Sydney.

By day four I needed time and space away from the on-field carnage and traded a morning at the cricket ground for a rare chance to gaze upon the waterfront. To avoid the heartache of watching the last morning's play I decided to revisit the Sydney Harbour Bridge. It had been ten years since my last visit to Sydney and in those backpacker days, I had climbed to the 134-metre summit with my sister, Alice. But this time I would not be paying hundreds of dollars for the privilege of climbing to the top as part of an organised climb. Instead, I would walk across the bridge for free, along the eastern footpath, just like hundreds do every day.

From Circular Quay I joined locals and tourists on board one of the iconic ferries and within minutes all thoughts of the latest cricket score diminished as we passed within metres of Sydney Opera House, its white sailed roof gleaming in the early sunshine. I disembarked at Luna Park and stared past the grotesque clown's face where holidaymakers queued patiently for a turn on the sideshows. There was no need to visit the House of Fun as I knew there would be plenty of comical antics that afternoon at the cricket ground, both on and off the pitch. The skyline was now dominated by the iconic bridge, its huge buttress and formidable steel columns rising from the choppy waters.

Sydney Harbour Bridge

From Luna Park I ventured towards Milsons Point, leaving behind the sounds of children's laughter as I searched for the paved steps that led onto the bridge. For some reason I envisaged the walkway to be a local secret, but this myth was quickly diminished with the realisation that visitors from across the world had already discovered the budget solution to awe-inspiring views. Amongst the steady flow of power walkers, joggers, transient office workers and backpackers I heard accents from across the globe.

As I gazed through the safety railings at the expansive views of Sydney Harbour and the Opera House, I thought back to my earlier climb when our guide shared a story about a worker called Vincent Kelly. He had fallen 60 metres from the bridge and survived by breaking the water tension with his spanner. On the other side of the city, I sensed the English cricketers were plunging towards defeat and no amount of luck would save them.

My phone beeped and then displayed the latest score, momentarily distracting me from embracing the stunning views. Far below, a flotilla of boats, ferries and cargo ships churned through the bay, their wakes forming long white streaks on the rippled surface.

At the end of the path I scanned the rafters for bridge climbers and located the next group as they walked steadily along the backbone of the bridge. They would soon be standing at the peak, their ant-like silhouettes standing proud against the bright sky. I turned my gaze away and strode purposely towards the end of the walkway, eager for a celebratory pint of ale, and found myself at the heritage listed Australian Pub. The clientele were subdued and not interested in cricket so I shared the bar and widescreen TV with the barman. There was no escaping the score as I drank the welcome beer. Cook was already out and it was clear I needed to quickly find a cab, to witness the final moments at the ground.

Once inside, I inched through the packed arena, drawn towards the red and white banners of the Barmy Army. Despite their team's imminent collapse the supporters chanted enthusiastically, until the final wicket remained. I once read that the orchestra continued to play as the Titanic tilted sharply and began its final slide into the icy waters of the Atlantic Ocean. Maybe it's an English trait to stare down disaster with a last waltz.

In the last few seconds, a hush descended over the

arena. Something was happening. You could feel the tension amongst the testosterone and sweat. Somewhere amidst the fluttering St Georges flags a lone trumpet player began to play. As the melodic sound of *Jerusalem* reverberated through the historic stadium the distinct smack of ball on willow carried across the humid air. The ball spun high into the clear sky and was plucked with assured confidence by Michael Clarke. The Australian crowd leapt as one, roared in applause and drowned out the stirring sounds of the trumpet. The Ashes were over.

16

THE PRICE OF IRON ORE

"The pay is good and I can walk to work."
John F. Kennedy
2013. Pilbara, Western Australia.

While living in England I encountered most form of transportation during my trips to work, including bikes, trains and cars. I even tried cross-country skiing to the Vauxhall Car Plant one morning, when a wintry whiteout closed all the roads. In Australia, you get used to travelling vast distances. Even going for milk normally warrants a car trip, as new shopping centres continually erode the need for local corner shops.

It is estimated that eight per cent of the Australian population fly to work and for three years I joined this genre. China's insatiable demand for resources has created opportunities in the North West, as large tracts of land is mined for its iron ore, transported overland to Port Hedland and then shipped to Asia.

Iron ore surface mining

Thousands of workers are required on these sites, to extract, process and ship the ore and most fly to an area known as the Pilbara. Once there, they live in purpose-built camps on the edge of the mine and work twelve hour shifts. Australians have termed this style of working as FIFO, meaning Fly In Fly Out.

After three years of living out of a holdall, working 8 days on and 6 days off it was time for me to quit. The lucrative money paid for working in remote locations for long periods comes at a price. My boys were growing quickly and I felt disconnected from their lives. My social life imploded, as I was rarely around for functions and my distance from Fran meant we spent more time texting than holding hands. Although the experience had been amazing, the detrimental effects on home life were too crucial to ignore and with a touch of sadness I knew it was time to finish. During my final weeks I studied the FIFO workers at Perth airport and decided to write an article about them.

The Gecko

The early morning queue for freshly ground coffee has grown longer in recent years as a new genre of traveller makes themselves comfortable in the frequent flyer lounges at Perth airport. Known as FIFO workers, these Fly In Fly Out miners now make up eight percent of the Australian workforce and spend over half their lives living in remote purpose-built villages at the edge of each mine site. A decade ago there was a small number of miners marching across the carpets in steel toe-capped boots, but brightly dressed resource workers are no longer a novelty in business lounges. Their zesty work shirts dazzle under the subdued neon as they join the white collar fraternity for a share of freshly ground coffee before departure.

First in line for coffee is a businessman, dressed in a designer shirt, tailored trousers and soft leather shoes. He taps quickly on his smart phone while one barista froths milk and another grinds coffee for the next customer, a Gen Y female, dressed in a bright yellow work shirt emblazoned with a wide fluorescent band across the middle. Miners, it seems, are hard to miss these days.

Her jeans are clean but no amount of scrubbing can erase the red dirt engrained in the dense fibres and her scuffed brown boots clash with the classic cut of the black polished shoes worn by the businessman. I watch as the coffee queue lengthens. It is filled with a mixture of resource workers and those on business.

The next miner is a Maori, who gives robust high fives to passing friends as they head to the buffet for breakfast. Behind him is a young girl with damp blonde hair, who clasps a paperback book and hides her eyes behind wrap-around sunglasses. On her back is a small rucksack emblazoned with the words, "Safety Comes First."

Two more miners are in the coffee queue. One is tall, with cropped hair and piercing eyes that never seem to leave his phone. He shuffles forward, avoiding conversation with passers-by, oblivious to the final miner to join the queue. This one is short and stocky, with a shock of dark hair and brown eyes. On the front of his shirt is the logo of a specialised contract company. Not all workers enjoy regular shift rosters and this man is heading to the north west of Australia for a specific task.

Apart from the Maori calling out animated greetings with each high five, the only sounds permeating from the plush lounge are the monotone announcements for the next flight departures. The destinations displayed on the flight board are a mixture of Australian landmark cities and remote mine sites. The Gold Coast is called out and a small party of excited backpackers jump up from nearby seats. A final call for Melbourne is announced and the businessman waiting for his cappuccino looks around at the screen, checks his watch and smiles awkwardly at the flustered barista.

Within a few hours, those at the coffee queue will be dispersed throughout the country, but what happens to mine workers once they step through the departure gate? We board on time but take off late and no one seems surprised. Our pilot apologies for the delay, due to heavy congestion, but I don't sense too many passengers being upset.

Within seconds of being airborne I gaze below at the remotest city in the world, Perth, Western Australia. Basking on the fringes of the Indian Ocean and cut in two by the wide meandering banks of the Swan River, this once tranquil city is now at the epicentre of a resources and energy boom. The plane banks right and crosses over the city centre, where new skyscrapers twinkle in the first rays of sunlight, the tallest belonging to resource giants and the banking sector.

While early starters begin another day of corporate life in the city, I wonder if they are aware of their work colleagues flying overhead. For a brief moment I glimpse at the cranes in Fremantle harbour and catch a sight of the elongated outline of Perth's playground, Rottnest Island. The Indian Ocean is a rich blue, peppered with sail boats and rows of cargo ships waiting in line for the call from the Fremantle quartermaster.

The pilot dips the wings and we turn north, following Perth's sprawling suburbs, which cling to the lucrative shoreline.

New housing estates are etched into the western fringe of the continent, but they eventually give way to scrubland and the pilot banks again, this time into the arid interior. We fly above dried riverbeds, carved by seasonal rains over millennia and if I look closely can make out the fickle remains of dirt tracks where off-road enthusiasts still explore. But many window blinds on the aircraft are pulled down. Most passengers have seen it all before and although the enthusiastic crew serve a basic but palatable breakfast, many on the flight are tempted to sleep rather than eat.

I prise open the vacuum packed foil and work my way through an overheated egg and bacon roll. While scrutinising the wrapper for the amount of preservatives that have masked any natural flavour, I take a peek at the well-groomed flight crew. Where is the glamour in air travel when most of the passengers are subdued by the thought of work rather than excited by the notion of a holiday? Are the stewardesses in training for international assignments, or is flying resource workers a convenient career for those that prefer to be home each evening, instead of being en route to a stopover in Kuala Lumpur?

The pilot prepares us for landing and we lose height steadily, revealing much more than a featureless desert. We are above the Pilbara, a vast area still inhabited by small settlements of Aboriginals, the traditional owners of the parched land. Some work in the nearby mines and Aboriginal elders continually negotiate with new mining companies wishing to extract the abundant natural resources locked beneath the red earth. Billions of tonnes have been discovered across an area larger than Europe, with China driving the demand to locate and extract the precious minerals.

The immense landscape is filled with small ridges, their crinkled tops emblazoned in fiery creases and the red dirt is partially hidden by a patchwork of lime green spinifex clinging to the crimson soil. As the plane banks for the final time I get my first sighting of mining activity. A dozer clears foliage on the outer fringes of the tenement, preparing the selected area for drilling and blasting. In the distance I can see the active mining area, where tiny yellow trucks trundle along dirt roads with their precious cargo. From a thousand feet, the trucks are Tonka toys, but up close and personal they are taller than my garage and have a payload of 150 tonnes. With high iron ore prices, the Pilbara is a lucrative area to do business, if you can manage operating costs.

Mine site runway

The airport is a simple affair. There is one landing strip with a row of air-conditioned tin sheds, modified for

use as waiting rooms and a passenger check in terminal. After a perfect landing we thank the flight crew then step into bright sunshine. As I cross the tarmac, persistent flies buzz across my face and a thin bead of sweat forms at the back of my neck as I wave them away. The tall man from the coffee queue heads straight to the entrance, where his personal assistant is waiting in the only clean four-wheel drive in the car park. He is the mine manager, ultimately responsible for all issues associated with safety, production and the environment and will be keen to meet his management team for the first meeting of the week.

The remaining passengers collect their luggage, then board the bus to the mining village and queue silently for room keys. With no food available in the active mine, they then head to the canteen to prepare their own meals where the array on offer is diverse and seemingly unlimited. Fresh salads, cold meats and bowls of fruit compete with biscuits, cakes and meat pies. As we leave the eatery, the blackboard for the evening meal is being written up by the head chef. Pepper steak, Cajun chicken and vegetable lasagne are tonight's specials.

Once outside in the heat, the miners finally find their voices. The subdued conversations during the flight are forgotten as they banter with workmates while boarding the waiting bus, which is plastered in thick red dirt from recent downpours. The bus departs for the active mine, sending a thin cloud of red dust into the humid air as the operators inside prepare to replace those on the opposite shift. After a safety brief, these men and women will soon be driving some of the largest mining trucks in the world capable of carrying hundreds of tonnes of ore.

The Gen Y girl walks past carrying a plastic bag filled with food and climbs into a waiting four-wheel drive.

Her world revolves around ore quality and a meeting is planned with stakeholders across the supply chain. Within thirty minutes she will be in a conference call with head office, talking to colleagues in one of the skyscrapers she flew past hours ago. Decisions made in this meeting can affect the quality of the iron ore heading to customers across the globe and unseasonal rains could impact the weekly forecast unless managed tightly.

The last in the coffee queue was a contractor, bought in for specialised work. At Perth airport he was a quiet, unassuming man, with a mop of black hair and broad shoulders. I spot him at midday abseiling down the side of the largest ore processing plant in the southern hemisphere. His task is to fit a crane gantry onto the side of the structure and after an extensive safety brief, he is now swinging by a rope and drilling holes thirty metres from the ground.

Construction worker

By now the sun is high and the ground tremors as the gigantic ore processing facility continually crushes, grinds and screens the iron ore, resulting in huge stockpiles awaiting the next train arrival. These trains are some of the longest and heaviest in the world, capable of carrying 32,000 tonnes during their five hour excursion to the nearby town of Port Hedland. From here, cargo ships transport hundreds of thousands of tonnes each week to the steel mills in China.

By sunset the miners from the dayshift crew are winding down. The mine manager heads for dinner and the Maori is on his way to the gym. The specialised contractor is sitting outside his room telling bedtime stories to his children 1200 km away while the Gen Y girl enjoys a sociable beer in the wet mess with colleagues. Long wooden tables are filled with beer bottles as miners, sit alongside each other, their yellow shirts now stained with sweat and tinged with red dirt.

For a few hours the mess is a boisterous hall filled with laughter and music. But by 9pm the bar will be silent. Rules are strict and every employee will be breath-tested for alcohol in the morning. I amble through the mining village towards a walking track that leads me into untouched country and very soon the noise and lights are forgotten as I gaze into the heart of the Milky Way.

On fly in day I am too fatigued to search for shooting stars and after a brief walk along the track, return to the cabin that I call home. A small green lizard is clinging to the mesh on my door and as I crouch lower to take a photo my mobile phones rings. The signal is weak and the boys are singing in the background. I hear something from Fran about an oil leak from the car and she lets slip that while home I forgot to repair the garden gate and it's now hanging on one hinge. These are things that can wait until I return but what affects me more is hearing that our boys need help with homework and despite her chirpy demeanour, her voice sounds drained.

I know why. Her mum and dad are very sick, I am out of reach for eight days, the boys are very young and it's clear my job as a FIFO employee needs to end. I say goodnight to Fran and the boys and turn out the light in my cabin. Outside I can hear the resident gecko scrambling across the hot tin roof. I fall asleep listening to his nocturnal scurrying and sense it won't be long before I'm home for good.

17

MICRO ADVENTURES

"Go and sleep on a hill and jump in a river before breakfast."
Alastair Humphries
2015. Busselton, Western Australia.

Twelve years after moving to Australia I still have moments where I could drop everything and permanently return to the UK. Newfound friends tell me that it will pass, but a recent trip home unsettled me. It wasn't just about being with family and close friends again. It was all the other things that I rediscovered, or had taken for granted when living in England. During our six-week trip we explored Greek islands, ran along windswept beaches in West Ireland, enjoyed a ploughman's lunch at the oldest public house in England and played hide and seek in rolling fields of ripened wheat on warm summer evenings. It was so surreal it felt like a dream. And I knew it was just a holiday. The weather would change, and the rains would return. They always did. Isn't that why so many people move from the UK to Australia? To escape the grey skies and damp.

The trip home had been an amazing experience, but it left me feeling edgy as we boarded the return flight to Australia. It was like I had two lives. The one in England surrounded by family and close friends, then across to Ireland for more of the same. I was leaving these people behind, but for what? The life we have chosen is on the western edge of Australia, in a popular seaside town, where children are free to explore, the ocean is enticing and the locals are friendly.

Since returning from Europe I have tried to look at what I have got, not what is missing and have attempted to reconnect with Australia in an effort to see what made the country so appealing a decade earlier. A combination of shoulder injuries, lethargy, numerous job changes, working away, university studies, young children, and terminal illnesses to in-laws had taken its toll. My aluminum boat had become neglected, the family kayak was rarely used, my walking boots were home to a family of field mice, and our tent sat idle in the shed.

While convalescing from a shoulder operation I discovered a book called Micro Adventures by the British explorer Alastair Humphries and began to appreciate that fun escapades were still possible without the need for major travel. I was living within 2 km of the Indian Ocean and across from my front door were extensive wetlands teeming with wildlife.

As my shoulder healed, I began to look at Australia through fresh eyes. My inaugural micro adventure was a sunset kayak trip around the longest wooden jetty in the Southern Hemisphere. At 1.8 km, it juts far into the Indian Ocean, and is no longer used for mooring cargo boats but is now a tourist attraction for thousands of visitors each year. After being flattened by a cyclone in 1978, the jetty underwent massive refurbishment and is a major tourist attraction in the south west of Australia. You can walk along it, fish from it, jump from it, snorkel or dive in the waters below it and even take a train to an underwater observatory at the end.

My quest was to paddle solo around the jetty at sunset and the timing was perfect. The heat of the day had dispersed and most people on the beach were enjoying sundowners as I walked past, dragging the kayak along the warm sand.

The calm waters of the bay were a kaleidoscope of rich blue and turquoise greens, stretching towards the hazy horizon. Dots of bright sunshine danced on every ripple and from across the wide bay I could hear the teenage screams of jetty jumpers as they plunged into the clear warm waters. As I sat astride the kayak a lone stingray glided past, trawling the shoreline for scraps of bait left behind by fishermen. The bay was alive with movement, colour and sound and as the sun plunged towards the cape peninsula, the wispy clouds flushed crimson and pink.

While photographers gathered at the water's edge to capture the sunset, I launched into the tranquil water, the sun low to my left and paddled hard to catch sight of the children on the jumping platform. They had been there all afternoon. A boisterous group of youngsters cajoling each other to attempt somersaults and star jumps into the azure waters. In the final minutes of daylight they were subdued and huddled together, glistening and giggling, their gangly shapes silhouetted by the late summer sun.

As I paddled below them, a lone jumper broke from the group and leapt from the jetty, his toned body perfectly straight as he plunged silently into the deep water. I wanted to stay and watch the others, but the sea was no longer glassy and the light was fading fast. The sun dropped below the horizon at the half-way point, just as the wind picked up and changed direction. It was now coming from the south and felt cool on my face, reminding me that autumn would soon grace these shores.

I was nearly 2 km offshore, and completely alone as small feisty waves continually broke across the bow of the kayak. My repaired shoulder was complaining of overuse but I ignored the stabbing pains and scanned the water, hoping to think of something else instead. That's when I remembered about the Great White shark sighting a week earlier. The paper had said that the shark swam under the jetty, then headed north and disappeared. Which is where I now bobbed in the last of the light. A local surfer had recently been taken by a shark in a nearby town and the continual sightings of sharks in the bay had been the biggest community topic all summer.

I was paddling back to shore now, directly into the wind. Far ahead, I could see the dimmed lights of the Goose Beach Bar, knowing that inside the funky exterior there would be visitors from across the world enjoying cocktails, tapas and boutique beers. The thought of sharks had spooked me. I wanted to be back on shore but fought off all negative thoughts to enjoy the final moments. My left shoulder weakened, causing me to slow as the beach drew nearer. A dark shape, long and wide, crossed my bow just below the water line. It could have been floating seaweed, a resident stingray, or shadows cast by my imagination. My heart was pounding and without thought, I twisted my torso to scan the waters behind me. The spontaneous motion pitched the kayak, just as a rogue wave ploughed into the side. It pitched awkwardly and I stabbed out the paddle blade in desperation, smacking it hard onto the water. The kayak responded, allowing me to steady myself, before ploughing forward.

To my left, a dorsal fin broke the surface, then sliced through the waves and as I blinked away the ocean spray, it was gone. My stomach knotted as I paddled hard towards the lights of the café, convinced it was a dolphin, but afraid that it wasn't. I focused on land and pumped my arms, knowing that each paddle stroke would propel me towards shallower water. As I approached the jumping platform, I kept my eyes locked onto the foreshore. The jetty jumpers would be home now, replaced by hardier souls. Nightfall was a time for fishermen and they would now be sitting at the end of the jetty, hoping to catch squid, crabs, herring or gummy shark.

It was dark when the kayak scraped its hull along the deserted beach. I dragged it away from the water, dropped my paddle and fell to the ground. While lying on the sand, I sucked greedily on the night air, gazed into space and thought about my next adventure. Once again, I felt excited about living in Australia.

18

AUTHORS NOTE

I hope you enjoyed these short stories and would be extremely grateful if you could share the word to others that are contemplating a trip to Australia. Most helpful of all, would be an honest review on Amazon. It should just take a few moments and as a new author, would be really appreciated.

If you do make it to Australia, I hope you have an amazing adventure.

Happy travels,
Alistair

19

ABOUT ALISTAIR

I grew up in a council estate, in an industrial town called Luton, 30 miles north of London. Like many parents in the community, mine were born overseas and moved to England in search of work. With an Irish mum, Scottish dad and five excitable children there were rarely any dull moments in our animated household.

Summer holidays were spent in Ireland and these were special times. We would build haystacks in the meadows, play on tractors, dig for cockles, run along windswept beaches and explore the wild landscape. Each evening, my Dad would seek out a corner of my Uncles Pub and we would sit and listen to fiddle players and musicians from across Ireland. When the music stopped, it was time for my Great Uncles, Barney and Francis to entertain the patrons. They were Seanachaís (Irish storytellers) and would enthral visitors to Donegal with their animated tales of life in rural Ireland.

The tradition of storytelling in my family lives on to this day. My brothers are apt at reciting their adventures to large audiences and being somewhat shyer, I have opted to write stories instead of telling them!

Dad was in the Merchant Navy and it was his tall tales about life on the seven seas that planted the first seeds of wanderlust in me. 48 countries later, there are still so many places I yearn to explore with my family.

After moving from England, Fran and I initially settled in the suburbs of Perth, Western Australia. We then moved south with our two children, in search of a country town by the Indian Ocean and discovered Busselton, the events capital of Western Australia.

When not kayaking around the longest jetty in the southern hemisphere, you might find me fishing in the pristine waters of Geographe Bay with my family.

Busselton is the gateway to the Margaret River Winery Region; a biodiversity hot spot, filled with rolling vineyards, world-class surf breaks, ancient forests and stunning beaches.

Alistair's journey continues @ www.alistairmcguinness.com

20

GAP YEAR TRAVEL

What happened to Alistair and Fran between leaving England and arriving in Australia?

While their visa was being processed, they travelled through Ecuador, Peru and Bolivia. Their next stop was Africa, for an overland adventure from Kenya to Cape Town. During their travels, Alistair kept a diary, which was converted into an adventure travel book.

It is called, Half a World Away: Searching for a Gap Year Travel Adventure.

Reviews

Mik Scarlet, BBC presenter. *"With wit and charm Alistair paints a picture of the joys and perils of backpacking. A must read..."*

Sue Magee, The Bookbag. *"An inspiring, enlightening and thoroughly readable story of the journey of a lifetime.*

Printed in Poland
by Amazon Fulfillment
Poland Sp. z o.o., Wrocław